Cultural Management

This shortform book tells the research story of cultural management, helping scholars to analyse and combine theoretical models into an approach of their own.

Cultural management emerged and developed out of the field of arts management in the 1980s, which imported managerial techniques and assumptions from mainstream commercial business into the arts. In the late 1990s, the field integrated entrepreneurial approaches to management in the creative industries before adapting to a new model, based on user experiences and co-creation. These historical phases are theorised respectively as cultural management 1.0, cultural management 2.0 and cultural management 3.0. Yet they also overlap. Bringing together theories of management and creativity, this book enables scholars to get a grip on the underlying assumptions and conditions which lie behind an eclectic and evolving field.

The author, an established expert in this field, empowers scholars and reflective practitioners to develop their own approach to cultural management, drawing on the available approaches, and to recognise that successful cultural management is contingent on understanding the context (organisational and personal) within which these models will be applied.

Chris Bilton is Reader in Creative Industries at the Centre for Cultural and Media Policy Studies at the University of Warwick, UK.

State of the Art in Business Research
Series Editor: Geoffrey Wood

Recent advances in theory, methods and applied knowledge (alongside structural changes in the global economic ecosystem) have presented researchers with challenges in seeking to stay abreast of their fields and navigate new scholarly terrains.

State of the Art in Business Research presents shortform books which provide an expert map to guide readers through new and rapidly evolving areas of research. Each title will provide an overview of the area, a guide to the key literature and theories and time-saving summaries of how theory interacts with practice.

As a collection, these books provide a library of theoretical and conceptual insights, and exposure to novel research tools and applied knowledge, that aid and facilitate in defining the state of the art, as a foundation stone for a new generation of research.

Comparative Corporate Governance
A Research Overview
Thomas Clarke

Brands and Consumers
A Research Overview
Jaywant Singh and Benedetta Crisafulli

Emergency Services Management
A Research Overview
Paresh Wankhade and Peter Murphy

Cultural Management
A Research Overview
Chris Bilton

For more information about this series, please visit: www.routledge.com/State-of-the-Art-in-Business-Research/book-series/START

Cultural Management
A Research Overview

Chris Bilton

Routledge
Taylor & Francis Group

LONDON AND NEW YORK

First published 2023
by Routledge
4 Park Square, Milton Park, Abingdon, Oxon OX14 4RN

and by Routledge
605 Third Avenue, New York, NY 10158

Routledge is an imprint of the Taylor & Francis Group, an informa business

British Library Cataloguing-in-Publication Data
A catalogue record for this book is available from the British Library

Library of Congress Cataloging-in-Publication Data
Names: Bilton, Chris, author.
Title: Cultural management : a research overview / Chris Bilton.
Description: Abingdon, Oxon ; New York, NY : Routledge, 2023. |
Includes bibliographical references and index.
Identifiers: LCCN 2022056484 (print) | LCCN 2022056485 (ebook) |
ISBN 9780367443429 (hardback) | ISBN 9781032490724 (paperback) |
ISBN 9781003009184 (ebook)
Subjects: LCSH: Creative ability in business. | Management.
Classification: LCC HD53 .B5528 2023 (print) |
LCC HD53 (ebook) | DDC 658.4/063–dc23/eng/20221129
LC record available at https://lccn.loc.gov/2022056484
LC ebook record available at https://lccn.loc.gov/2022056485

ISBN: 978-0-367-44342-9 (hbk)
ISBN: 978-1-032-49072-4 (pbk)
ISBN: 978-1-003-00918-4 (ebk)

DOI: 10.4324/9781003009184

Typeset in Times New Roman
by Newgen Publishing UK

Contents

Illustrations

Figures

Table

Preface

The idea for this book was inspired by Pier Luigi Sacco's concept of 'Culture 3.0' (Sacco et al. 2018). My time frame (roughly 1980 to the present) does not map onto Sacco's, which considers the dynamics of supply and demand in European culture over centuries, nor have I modelled my argument directly on Sacco's three 'regimes of value creation'. However, there are some common concerns, notably Sacco's concept of Culture 3.0, 'culture as collective sense-making', in which production and distribution of culture have been democratised, and networks and communities are driving culture rather than individuals. This got me thinking about how cultural managers have had to adapt over time to different models of culture.

Sacco argues that Culture 1.0 was primarily driven by individuals and was dominated by 'the arts' rather than by industrial modes of production. Although latterly this did evolve into industrial models of production for mass audiences, for example, the nineteenth-century novel, the arts were a disposable luxury, not a public good. Culture 2.0 describes the commercial, profitable cultural industries – the model here was Hollywood and United States 'mass media', a reaction against the 'artistic' traditions of Europe. Culture 2.0 was more responsive to fans and fan cultures, capitalising on the possibilities of mass production and mass audiences. Finally, as noted above, culture 3.0 shifted the focus away from artistic or industrial models of production towards 'content communities', made possible by new technologies of production and consumption, in which 'everybody is creative' and culture and media products become pervasive. Culture thus becomes part of our everyday lives, echoing Lash and Urry's 'culturalisation' thesis in which 'ordinary manufacturing industry is becoming more and more like the production of culture' (Lash and Urry 1994, 123), and Mike Featherstone's postmodern blurring of aesthetic culture and social cultures, 'the aestheticization of everyday life' (Featherstone 2007).

How could managers respond to these different forms of culture? In the first chapter, I will introduce my three modes of cultural management – 1.0, 2.0, 3.0 – following a historical trajectory starting with the professionalisation of arts management in the 1980s, through the entrepreneurial rhetoric of 'creative industries' at the turn of the millennium, leading to a new rhetoric of co-creation, fan cultures and participatory culture, a symptom and a driver of today's platform capitalism.

Subsequent chapters take each of these models of cultural management in turn, showing how different approaches to management – entrepreneurial, strategic, controlling, laissez-faire – map onto different assumptions and definitions of culture.

It is worth emphasising that this historical framing is quite approximate – actually these different models overlap and coexist. The final chapter shows how different approaches to leadership could usefully be deployed to different stages in the innovation process. In other words, whilst different models of management and leadership have evolved in response to changing social and economic circumstances, the transitions are not clear-cut and can be combined eclectically to fit the needs of the project.

Along the way I have tried to highlight different theories of management and creativity and consider the assumptions which lie behind them and their potential applications. This is not primarily a theoretical book, but it does attempt to lay out concepts and strategies which could be applied to real scenarios (and to the ways in which cultural management is taught). In keeping with the Routledge book series, the book compresses a lot of material into a small space – this might mean some nuances and complexities have been lost and I have tried to avoid deep dives into theory or protracted case studies of practice. Hopefully this can be a useful primer to the range of thinking available about cultural management which is available to all of us – researchers, students, practitioners. Once you have oriented yourself, you may decide to dive deeper into some of the literature about management, culture and creativity, or to explore how theories can be applied and changed through practice in your own experience.

References

Featherstone, M. (2007). *Consumer Culture and Postmodernism*. London: Sage.

Lash, S. and Urry, J. (1994). *Economies of Signs and Space*. London: Sage.

Sacco, P.L., Ferilli, G. and Tavano Blessi, G. (2018). From Culture 1.0 to Culture 3.0: Three socio-technical regimes of social and economic value creation through culture, and their impact on European Cohesion Policies. *Sustainability*, *10*(11), p. 3923.

Acknowledgements

Thank you to Terry Clague at Routledge for initiating this book, and to Naomi Round Cahalin and her colleagues for helping turn it into a reality. As this is a book about cultural management, I thank all managers who have inspired and influenced me: Vikki Heywood and Michael Boyd at the Royal Shakespeare Company; Tony Wilson (RIP), the archetypal maverick entrepreneur at Granada, Factory and all things Manchester; Heather Maitland for teaching me about marketing; Dave Wilson for teaching me that management can be creative too. And my friend and former colleague Oliver Bennett for managing me.

Thanks to my colleagues and students at the University of Warwick: Ruth Leary for teaching me about creativity, and later about intellectual property law; Jo Garde-Hansen and the MCI students for helping me develop the 'Leading for Innovation' chapter, and thanks to Matt Peacock for talking to us about vulnerable leadership and social change.

On the home front, thanks to Rich, Bruce and the Gipsy Queen for inspiration and chat. And the biggest thanks of all to Anna Wright, without whom nothing at all would be possible.

1 A very short history of cultural management

What is cultural management? The idea is contentious. On the one hand, *cultural* management might be a form of special pleading, exempting artists and arts managers from the rules and norms which govern other organisations. On the other hand, cultural *management* might be an imposition of commercial, managerial logic onto aesthetic practice. Turning to academic research, is there any coherent body of canonical texts, agreed 'best practice' or historical timeline which could chart the emergence of cultural management as a discipline? Cultural management seems more like a hybrid, drawing eclectically on a range of disciplines including cultural studies, management studies, social theory.

This book will take these contradictions and uncertainties as a starting point. Dividing cultural management into three phases or tendencies will allow the reader to focus on three particular challenges of cultural management. But as will become clear, this is a way of structuring a short book, not a definitive history. The 'stages' overlap and the dilemmas recur. At the core of cultural management is a paradox – the aesthetic and social values of artistic production and culture come up against the economic values of business management and efficiency. This dilemma has been addressed in different ways, but never resolved. The aim of this book is to help the reader navigate some of the assumptions and values which lie behind different iterations of cultural management in order to plot an independent course.

Cultural Management 1.0

The prehistory of cultural management could take us back to the impresarios and showmen of the nineteenth century in America or Europe (DiMaggio 1986), or further back to the patronage of the arts by church, state and commerce in Renaissance Europe (Negus and Pickering 2004). It should also acknowledge a wider set of practices

DOI: 10.4324/9781003009184-1

beyond Europe and America, in China, India, the Middle East and Africa, traditions and values which continue to challenge the dominant Western paradigms of cultural management and cultural policy (Hua 2018; Şuteu 2006; Lee and Lim 2014).

This book's shorter history of 'cultural management' begins with the application of management principles to Western cultural organisations and practices in the 1980s.

The reason for starting here is the emergence of arts management as an academic discipline from the 1970s onwards (Deveraux 2018, 7–8). At around this time, postgraduate courses in the UK at City University and in the United States at New York's New School (and at UCLA) were directed at a new cadre of professional arts managers. This signalled the emergence of cultural management as a viable career – it now became possible to pursue cultural management as a profession in its own right, rather than as the extension of a pre-existing career as an artist or (less commonly) as a manager from outside the sector.

Previous generations of self-taught cultural entrepreneurs, Hollywood moguls, actor-managers, record company bosses, hucksters and showmen had not felt the need for any specialised training. However, the increasing importance of public subsidy for arts organisations brought with it a demand for professional expertise and accountability. This in turn created an opportunity for universities, training providers and consultants to codify a set of methods and principles, signalling the emergence of arts management and its subsequent variant, 'cultural management'. And no doubt education, specifically higher education, plays a key role in legitimising professional status.

From the beginning there were significant variations in definition. In the UK, the 'accountability' brought by public funding was tempered by an emphasis on entrepreneurial resourcefulness as that same public funding was reduced. British cultural management was accordingly linked to the business schools with a more entrepreneurial slant. In the United States, cultural management was part of a bigger move towards professional management of non-profit organisations. One of the biggest funders of US cultural organisations through the 1960s, predating the federal National Endowment for the Arts and state and city-based funding programmes, was the Ford Foundation, cementing the marriage between the arts, not-for-profits and philanthropy. US cultural management continues to be linked to non-profit organisations, civil society and arts education programmes directed to the public good, rather than to profit. In France and Germany, where earned income is proportionately lower and public subsidy higher than the UK, cultural management was framed in terms of humanistic and civic values rather than economic logic. Universities and cultural organisations are part of the civic and regional infrastructure, and cultural management exists somewhere on a spectrum from technocratic pragmatism to reforming idealism.

The paradox at the core of cultural management is the claim that cultural products and processes are essentially unmanageable. This relates to Bourdieu's concept of 'symbolic goods', products whose meaning and hence value depends upon perception. If value is no longer intrinsic, but framed in the mind's eye of the receiver, cultural products are inherently unpredictable. Moreover, the creative processes and people behind these products are often considered to be similarly unmanageable – maverick, spontaneous, individualistic, intuitive and irrational.

The three stages of cultural management considered in this book address this paradox in different ways. In the early years of cultural management, or 'arts management' as it was known at the time, the opposition between artistic practice and management systems was sharply delineated. Confronted by this division, cultural managers could respond in one of two ways. Either they could impose assumptions and models imported from business 'best practice' upon the arts and demand compliance. Or they could accept their limitations and attempt to manage outcomes without intervening in the processes behind the product. I include both these approaches as part of 'Cultural Management 1.0'.

The defining characteristic of Cultural Management 1.0 is the separation between managerial and artistic processes. 'Management' in this case is concerned with structures and systems around but outside the creative process. The latter remains a 'black box' (Pratt 2017), which managers should fear to open. The best summary of this logic is Amabile's dictum of 'autonomy around process' (Amabile 1998). She argues that managers should set strategic goals and outcomes for a creative process or creative team – but avoid attempting to micro-manage the creative process itself. Whilst this affords the creative individual or team a measure of freedom, it also isolates them from the realities of the organisation. More damagingly, it imposes or reinforces hierarchies and divisions which can ultimately lead to resentments as well as sharpening inequalities (class, gender, ethnicity) which are already entrenched in the cultural sector. Yet for all its faults, it provides a level of security and comfort. Everybody knows their place and their role. Cultural Management 1.0 allows managers to manage and creators to create. It also highlights the role of those cultural intermediaries (administrators, managers, marketers, consultants) who were being encouraged by universities and policymakers to see cultural management as a viable career option during the 1980s and 1990s.

Cultural Management 2.0

'Cultural Management 2.0' describes a reconfigured relationship between culture and management in the late 1990s and early 2000s. The rebranding of cultural industries as 'creative industries' by the UK government in 1998 shifted focus from publicly funded 'arts' to commercially driven 'creative industries'. This sector had been neglected by the arts management programmes of the previous decades but now took centre stage in cultural policy. Whereas Cultural Management 1.0 recognised a contradiction between aesthetic culture and business management, Cultural Management 2.0 insisted on their synergy. Creativity was at the heart of this new relationship, a word devalued through overuse but increasingly valued by both a resurgent cultural sector and by commercial managers.

It is worth noting that 'creative industries' in the UK was a policy-driven construct, not a coherent sector. Talk to any creative worker over the past 25 years, and they are unlikely to say they work in the creative industries. They might claim to work in the film industry, the music business or in television or publishing. Nor would they necessarily acknowledge that their sector faces different challenges from any other business. At a 1999 consultation meeting with the newly established Department for Culture, Media and Sport (DCMS),[1] some industry representatives confided that they didn't know why they had been invited – they were more interested in discussing tax breaks with the Department of Trade and Industry than cultural policy with DCMS. Then as now, most cultural managers in the creative industries continue to be preoccupied by familiar problems facing any business – cashflow, tax, HR and marketing – rather than the policy discourse of creative industries.

According to government advisers (see below 'From cultural industries to creative industries'), the creative industries label was designed to appeal to the incoming government by signalling enterprise, renewal, freedom, choice – and to distance the New Labour government from the 'cultural industries' policies of the old Labour metropolitan councils of the 1980s. Whereas the Greater London Council had used the cultural industries to advance a progressive agenda of empowerment and social inclusion, the DCMS used 'creativity' to focus on economic transformation and individual self-expression.

'Enterprise culture' had been a theme of the Conservative national government in the 1980s (Keat and Abercrombie 1991). Now 'cultural entrepreneurship' and creative enterprise merged the rhetoric of self-made, independent entrepreneurs with the apparently endless possibilities of 'creativity', a resource with apparently no material costs and unlimited potential value through 'the generation and exploitation of intellectual property' (DCMS 1998).

At the same time as British cultural organisations and creative individuals were being nudged towards business enterprise, across the world business enterprises were exploring the possibilities of 'creative' management. The catalyst here was the arrival of digital technologies which disrupted traditional value chains (Porter 2001), also a continuation of the 'culturisation' thesis advanced by Lash and Urry (1994), the recognition that 'ordinary manufacturing industry is becoming more like the production of culture' (Lash and Urry 1994, 123). Faced with these two challenges, the radical unpredictability of discontinuous change and disruptive technologies, and the 'brandification' of manufacturing and service industries (Klein 2000) so that they too began to have an increasing reliance on 'symbolic' value, managers looked for 'creative' solutions. Creativity became a buzzword in business schools, an often vague term applied to everything from cars and software to sports (Tusa 2003). Creative management and creative strategy spread outwards from the creative industries to become the everyday currency of management.

Cultural Management 2.0 resolves the paradox of aesthetic and commercial values in the creative and cultural industries by arguing that these oppositions can be reconciled in a shared pursuit of creativity, entrepreneurship and innovation. This triptych has become a dominant theme not only in UK cultural policy and NGOs like National Endowment for Science, Technology and the Arts (NESTA), but also in cultural management curricula.

The UK definition of creative industries has proved popular with other national governments, not least because it fits with a neoliberal, individualistic political and economic system where risk-taking entrepreneurs replace state providers, and 'creativity' unlocks innovation and profit in the wider 'creative economy', not just within the so-called creative industries (Mould 2018). The blurring of categories (business + creativity = creative business) promises agency to creative individuals, taking control of their work and challenging the hegemony of both corporate and state monopoly. It also reflects the lived experience of many creative workers who are either self-employed individuals or working in micro-enterprises with fewer than ten employees. The reality of that experience (precarity, self-exploitation) may not reflect the promise of 'good work' (Wright 2018), and the entrepreneurial life may be 'forced' upon creative workers rather than chosen (Oakley 2014). But it reflects an entrepreneurial approach to cultural management which became dominant in the early 2000s.

The idea that culture and management form two balancing halves of an equation depends upon the assumption firstly that 'culture', and more specifically 'creativity', are essentially manageable and managed processes. Secondly, it is assumed that 'management' is not imposed hierarchically from above, but energised from below through entrepreneurship – and more particularly by 'creative' entrepreneurship of 'artrepreneurs' (Hagoort 2003). These two assumptions are at the core of Cultural Management 2.0.

Cultural Management 3.0

The third iteration of cultural management returns to one of the core properties of 'symbolic goods', the idea that the value of cultural products is co-created through consumption. In other words, value is relative and relational – what we think of a film or a piece of music will depend not only on who we are but who we are with at the time.

Digital tools and platforms promise to democratise distribution and production. Bearing in mind that the companies behind these tools and platforms are increasingly powerful and influential, this democratisation takes place within certain limitations. Nevertheless, fans, consumers and we-media play an increasingly central role not only in defining and recreating cultural value, but also in co-creating cultural products.

Jay Rosen's (2006) post describing 'The People Formerly Known as the Audience' marks the emergence of Cultural Management 3.0 (Rosen 2006). Whereas previously cultural management was concerned with cultural production, over the past 15 years cultural managers have become increasingly concerned with managing processes of cultural consumption.

Consumer behaviour, especially online, leaves a residue of data about consumer identities, described by Shoshana Zuboff (2019) as a 'behavioural surplus'. Some of the most powerful companies in the world aim to harvest this data and turn it into 'prediction products' which can be used to sell advertising, but also to manipulate purchasing decisions, even political decisions.

With some notable exceptions (Netflix, Amazon Prime), big tech companies like Facebook/Meta, Apple, Amazon, Google/Alphabet, Tencent, AliBaba are not investing in the management of cultural production or cultural products. Their business models depend upon the management of cultural consumption.

Amazon Prime's main value to Amazon is to lock in long-term customer relationships and deliver profit through future purchases

(Life-Time Value, or LTV). The majority of Amazon Prime members do not sign up specifically for the video streaming content, but for the shopping benefits. And whilst Amazon is notoriously secretive about its profits and revenues, various recent surveys of US households calculate that Amazon Prime members spend between three and four times as much per year as other Amazon users. For this reason, despite their investments in content creation (Apple TV, YouTube Originals), the big tech companies are mostly 'content agnostic' – they see content as a means to an end, a way of generating traffic and drawing down consumer data, not an end in itself. The other advantage of being 'content agnostic' is to maintain the fiction that tech platforms are not publishers, responsible for the content they produce, they are mere common carriers, like telecoms, providing a neutral space for other people's self-expression.

How do we 'manage' cultural consumption? Value is being co-created, so building strong relationships with consumers, and facilitating strong relationships between them, becomes part of the challenge. Of course customer relationships have always been important, but in a time of digital communication those relationships have become more widespread, frictionless and engaging. Participatory cultures, fandom, active audiences are likewise not new phenomena – but their impacts are accelerated and deepened by digital media (Jenkins 2006; Hills 2002). Big tech companies have built their business models around monetising these relationships, principally by harvesting consumer data and selling advertising. For content creators, the challenge now is to take back ownership of the customer relationship, restoring creative and media content and content creators to the centre of that relationship as something valuable rather than being something peripheral and incidental.

The networks and communities of cultural consumption are no longer simply receivers or amplifiers; they are part of the production cycle. Games which are 'modded' (modified, hacked) are turned into successful games in their own right; *League of Legends* began life as a fan mod of *Warcraft 3*. Meanwhile, E L James' popular fiction and film franchise *Fifty Shades of Grey* was first shared on the fanfiction.net community as an erotic reworking of characters in Stephenie Meyer's *Twilight* books. James then set up her own website and turned her fan fiction into a self-published novel which went on to attract the attention of a mainstream publisher and become a global bestseller. Trying to feed this kind of fan creativity back into the value of the original product has led many cultural businesses to sacrifice their concerns about copyright in order to mobilise their fans. By allowing the fan community to take control, publishers and broadcasters hope to tap into a richer source of cultural value than content alone.

Facilitating relationships requires something other than the hierarchical structures and systems of Cultural Management 1.0, or the creative, innovative entrepreneurs of Cultural Management 2.0. Instead managers have to be more responsive, adapting to the relationships with and between audiences, following emerging patterns instead of trying to predict them. This requires a measure of humility and perhaps vulnerability – acknowledging that the best ideas and the greatest value come from customers, not from innovative products. Our definition of creativity needs to extend beyond cultural production to encompass the co-creative ways in which products are experienced and valued. Our definition of cultural management needs to include a larger set of processes and interactions which extend beyond the point of origination and production. Managing these relationships and interactions will be considered in the fourth chapter of this book as Cultural Management 3.0.

Before considering different models of cultural management, we should pause to consider what kind of 'culture' is being managed. Specifically, over the period from the 1980s to the present, there have been two notable shifts in emphasis and meaning. The first was a shift in academic cultural studies during the 1980s from thinking about culture from the perspective of production towards a focus on cultural consumption. The second was a policy shift away from arts and culture towards 'creative industries' initiated by the UK government in 1998. We begin with changing concepts of culture in cultural studies.

What is culture? From production to consumption

Academic studies of cultural policy, which provide the theoretical underpinning for cultural management, are embedded in a range of disciplines, from urban geography (Pratt 2005; Scott 1999) to sociology (Hesmondhalgh, Peterson). Chief among these is cultural studies (Bennett 1998). Changing preoccupations of cultural studies, like shifts in cultural policy rhetoric, are closely aligned with changing approaches to cultural management.

Within the time frame considered during this chapter, the emergence of British cultural studies in the 1980s shifted focus from cultural production to cultural consumption. Previous mostly American scholarship had focused on the 'political economy' of the cultural industries, analysing how media ownership reinforced the hegemony of social and political elites (Schiller 1989; Mosco 2009; Gitlin 1980).

The Birmingham Centre for Cultural Studies considered how culture, especially popular culture, could be a site of counter-hegemony or 'resistance' (Hall et al. 1976). Whilst it was true that media content was imbued with reactionary political messages and either by accident or design tended to reinforce the values and beliefs of the dominant social class, nevertheless ordinary consumers could read against the grain of these messages. Decoding culture in their own terms, viewers of soap operas, readers of romantic fiction, wearers of high street fashion could enact little rebellions, in a 'subversive' reading of a text, even in the cut of a jacket's lapel (Hebdige 1979).

By drawing attention to the way consumption contexts add to the meaning and value of cultural content, British cultural studies laid the foundations for fan studies and the logic of culture 3.0. Cultural products, described by Bourdieu as 'symbolic goods', acquire their meaning through acts of interpretation by audiences, fans and users. Value is not intrinsic to the product, and meanings are not restricted to the meanings intended by the producer. Paying closer attention to communities of readers, viewers and consumers as the ultimate arbiters of cultural value would also have implications for cultural management.

Cultural studies helped to legitimise popular culture as serious and meaningful. Cultural marketing in the 1990s could be seen as an extension of audience studies in the 1980s. The support for popular forms like music, film and festivals under Britain's metropolitan councils in London, Manchester and Sheffield drew upon a cultural studies perception of popular culture as a site of resistance and counter-hegemony. When the Greater London Council threatened to turn London's South Bank arts complex into a 'people's palace', the dominance of white, middle class, male, heteronormative culture was called into question.

In the end, foregrounding popular culture did not result in a radical reordering of British cultural values. What Paul Willis described in 1990 as 'resistance through, not against, the market' (Willis 1990) was by the admission of its proponents, including Willis himself, a limited form of rebellion. The American cultural critic Thomas Frank (2001) went further, accusing academic cultural studies of facilitating the hegemony of neoliberal market-driven capitalism. The community arts movement, initially framed by the Arts Council of Great Britain in the 1970 Baldry Report as 'new activities', was absorbed under the heading of 'combined arts' and eventually handed over to regional arts funders, with the major arts institutions (most with the word 'Royal' or 'National' in their titles) continuing to absorb the major share of national arts funding. According to Owen Kelly, the community arts movement was bought off by the promise of funding and mainstream legitimacy and the threat to establishment values and institutions was derailed (Kelly 1984).

The legacy for cultural management was firstly a keener sense of audiences and the diversity and unpredictability of their responses and preferences. The value of cultural products depends also on the values of those who are consuming it. Cultural consumption is not passive; it is active and creative. Managers of cultural organisations needed to take a broader view of the processes of production and consumption, including what Bourdieu (1993) describes as the 'field' and 'habitus' of cultural production, or what systems theories of creativity refer to as the 'field' and 'domain'.

Secondly, the scope of what could legitimately be termed 'culture' extended beyond what had previously been termed 'the arts'. Commercial culture (TV, comics, popular music) was not innately inferior to the subsidised arts (theatre, opera, ballet). Attitudes and methods from the commercial sector could be selectively imported into 'arts management'.

Thirdly, some of the rebellious energy from Britain's metropolitan councils in the 1980s would later be absorbed into the New Labour government's 'creative industries' policies of 1998. As will be discussed below, the transition from 'cultural' to 'creative' industries cut creative expression off from its subversive, counter-cultural roots. The new government's vision focused on innovative, entrepreneurial creative individuals, not the shifting tectonic plates of class and culture beneath them. Nevertheless, opening out the definitions of what was culture and who could produce it would also challenge top-down assumptions about cultural management, expertise and excellence.

The Greater London Council was abolished in 1986. The Birmingham Centre for Cultural Studies was closed in 2002. Yet the ideas of creative consumption, of 'everyday creativity', of bottom-up demotic popular culture challenging elite institutions and notions of 'excellence' have taken on a new digital life. The theoretical context of cultural studies has been reinvigorated by fan studies and 'we-media'. All of this moves the dial away from studies of cultural production and cultural texts towards the contexts of cultural consumption, as the site where meaning and value are actively created.

What is culture? From cultural industries to creative industries

According to John Newbigin, one of the authors of the 1998 *Creative Industries Mapping Document*, the term 'creative industries' was more pragmatic than ideological.[2] Policy documents have to be marketed internally, towards building a consensus among policymakers, before they are directed externally to policy recipients. Seeking to build support for the government's attempt to place cultural/creative industries at the heart of economic and social transformation, 'creative industries' tapped into ideas of change and innovation which spoke to the New Labour brand. The term also implied wealth creation and individual freedom. Perhaps most importantly, 'creative industries' drew a line between the incoming New Labour government and the old Labour of the metropolitan councils, most notably the Greater London Council, which had linked 'cultural industries' policy to social inclusion, cultural diversity and social change (Bianchini 1987; Garnham 2005).

That change of wording might have seemed innocent or arbitrary to the consultants who instigated it – but it has been the subject of much debate among cultural policy researchers. The definition of creative industries as 'those industries which have their origin in individual creativity, skill and talent and which have a potential for wealth and job creation through the generation and exploitation of intellectual property' (DCMS 1998) remains controversial. First of all, the emphasis on 'individual' creativity skill and talent belies the collaborative nature of work in the creative industries. Secondly, whilst 'wealth and job creation' are undoubtedly one aspect of the creative industries, this is not their only or even primary objective. People working in the creative industries are driven by a variety of motives – self-expression, social issues, aesthetics, cultural tradition – and whilst they want to earn a living, the majority are unlikely to become wealthy nor to be commercially driven. A majority of creative and media businesses are self-employed sole traders or micro-businesses, with only a handful generating significant employment opportunities for others. Finally, 'generation or exploitation intellectual property' sets up a value chain in which content is created (generated), then sold (exploited). For that value chain to function, generation comes first, establishing a kind of hierarchy in which individual genius creators (talented, skilled, creative) are the engine of the new creative economy. Certain cultural activities and institutions which do not generate intellectual property, most notably heritage organisations like museums and galleries, community and participatory arts, amateur arts, festivals, musical theatre (or any theatre not presenting 'new' work) sat uneasily with this new definition.

At the same time, some activities which had previously been marginal to the 'cultural' industries now found themselves at the heart of the new creative industries. Chief amongst these was computer software, which included 'leisure software' (games) alongside more mundane applications, and is listed prominently in the 1998 document. The inclusion of this and other categories such as publishing and advertising boosted the statistics on income, GDP and employment for the sector as a whole. The emphasis on 'wealth and job creation' in the *Mapping Document* definition thus became self-fulfilling.

Whilst the UK was not the first country to use the term 'creative industries' (Australia can claim that honour), the DCMS definition has continued not only to be at the core of UK cultural policy, but increasingly influential around the world. What began as a parochial British matter, tweaking some words in a document to appeal to a particular audience, has changed the way cultural policymakers approach questions of funding, training and regulation for the sector.

From a cultural studies perspective, 'creative industries' disregarded the wider 'structure of feeling' (Williams 1971) which Raymond Williams described as lying behind cultural 'texts'. For Williams, 'culture' has a social and anthropological dimension as well as an aesthetic expression – the artefacts produced by the cultural industries are accordingly rooted in shared ideas and values, in community and class affiliations, and in a particular time and place. Seismic shifts in the underlying structure of feeling could throw up new cultural formations, and in this way an 'emergent' or 'residual' culture could challenge the dominant culture of the time (Williams 1977). According to Williams 'creativity', change and progress in the ideological and aesthetic realm were embedded in deeper cultural changes, not just individual skill and talent, and new ideas are often reiterations or combinations of old ones. This is the root of Williams' cultural materialism, a variation on Marxist theory, which proposed that material forces (economics and social relations) were not all-powerful, and that 'culture' could shape the world we live in as well as being shaped by it.

By removing this sense of connection to a specific material 'culture', the newly minted 'creative industries' drew focus away from collective experiences and values in order to suggest that creativity is the work of autonomous individuals. From a management perspective this has significant implications for how we organise and manage creative organisations and people.

Like the counter-cultural rhetoric of cultural studies in the 1980s, the rhetoric of creative industries has had a longer impact on attitudes to cultural management.

As will be discussed in Chapter 2, 'Cultural Management 1.0' assumes that creative processes and creative people are essentially unmanageable, simultaneously reinforcing and mitigating the myth of individual creative genius by isolating the creative individual and the moment of ideation from the managerial structures which surround them. The hierarchies and divisions of this management model pander to the romantic idea of artistic creativity disconnected from and ultimately transcending the material realities around them, cutting them loose from any rooted sense of time and place. This echoes the 'creative industries' logic of autonomous individualism.

Cultural Management 2.0 reconnects individual creativity to collective processes and embeds the moment of ideation into a longer sequence of development and realisation. Creativity is framed as a collective, multi-stage process involving different inputs and different people. Creative individuals are no longer placed outside or in opposition to management. There is then some sense of creative work taking place within a collective 'culture', albeit not driven by the kind of tectonic shifts in values and ideologies identified with Williams' 'structure of feeling'. At the same time the entrepreneurial logic of Cultural Management 2.0 resonates with the definition of creative industries based on 'wealth and job creation'. By integrating creative and managerial processes, Cultural Management 2.0 might reinforce the creative industries logic of accumulation.

Cultural Management 3.0 is a response to the relative, relational value of cultural products – meaning and value are always dependent on a social context, not only the time and place of reception but the social relationships around the receiver. What matters here is the culture of consumption rather than the culture of production – so this understanding of cultural relativism is different from Williams' 'structure of feeling' shaping the moment of conception. Again though, Cultural Management 3.0 seems more attuned to the collective logic of 'cultural industries' than the individualism of 'creative industries' (Garnham 2005).

Changing terminology of 'cultural' and 'creative' industries encourages us to reflect on the balance between the collective and the individual in creative processes and products. These differences are echoed in the different models of cultural management considered in this book. More recently, academic discourse has tended to favour the term 'cultural creative industries' – a compromise perhaps, but also acknowledging that the sector encompasses various sub-categories, some more individualistic or collective, some more or less commercially driven. In this version, the cultural/creative industries are represented as concentric circles radiating out from a creative core towards more commercial/less cultural businesses at the periphery (Throsby 2010, 26–27). That complexity is more representative of the reality of cultural management. Managing a museum will require a different approach from managing an advertising agency. 'Cultural/creative' may sound clumsy, but as will be discussed in Chapter 5 of this book, managers in the end must address the complex, overlapping realities of the cultural/creative sector. The more rigid categories of creative industries or cultural industries were always more ideological than real. That separation might be useful in framing cultural policy but, for cultural managers, the creative and the cultural are two sides of the same coin. Understanding and managing such paradoxes is part of the job.

Paradoxical thinking

This introduction has trailed three categories of cultural management which will be examined in more detail over the remainder of this book. Table 1.1 summarises some of the key features of each model. Before outlining the content of subsequent chapters, it's important to add a caveat to the schema developed so far.

A classification of cultural management in three parts might work in a Powerpoint presentation or a 'very short' introduction, but on closer examination the reality is likely to be more complex. The categories outlined in the table and in this book are overlapping, with different tendencies diverging and converging in different configurations in different industry sectors, organisational settings and projects. The point of separating them out historically is to consider that there is no perfect recipe for cultural management – the mix of ingredients will depend on external and internal factors, and historical context is one of these variables. Trying to apply a 1990s model of cultural management in the

Table 1.1 Three models of cultural management

	Cultural Management 1.0	*Cultural Management 2.0*	*Cultural Management 3.0*
Historical origins	1980s	Late 1990s	2010s +
Cultural context	The Arts	Creative Industries	Digital Media
Ideology	Paternalism	Enterprise	Democratisation
Creativity as …	Individual genius	Creative team/ system	Co-creation
Intervention as …	Laissez-faire	Managed process	Enabling
Leadership as …	Motivation	Coordination	Delegation
Management dilemma	Release vs. control	Entrepreneurship vs. strategy	Opening vs. orchestrating

2020s (or vice versa) is unlikely to work, but there still might be useful connections we can make with Cultural Management 1.0 in a Cultural Management 3.0 organisation (and vice versa).

Where the models can be useful is in addressing some of the paradoxes and contradictions of cultural management. Each model focuses on a different problem – motivation and autonomy, entrepreneurship and strategy, co-creation and authority – and must navigate a path between two opposing principles.

The idea of paradoxical thinking – keeping two contradictory ideas in play at the same time – draws on Arthur Koestler's theory of creativity as 'bisociation'. Koestler (1976) argued that creative thinking finds an unexpected connection between two habitually disconnected frames of reference. In so far as cultural management seeks to manage creative thinking, it must bridge between apparently opposing tendencies – between divergent and convergent thinking, between novelty and value, between spontaneous and rational decision-making. In order to manage these bisociative dualities, managers must make some creative connections of their own. In the following chapters, some of these contradictions and connections will be considered in more detail.

Chapter 2 will explore 'Cultural Management 1.0'. As noted above, Cultural Management 1.0 hinges on the opposition between 'unmanageable' artists on one hand and managerial methods imported from outside the cultural sector by a new professional cadre of cultural managers. Not surprisingly these early forays into cultural management stirred mutual suspicion between artists and managers. The solution to these problems was to separate out the artistic and managerial processes. Artists would be free to create in their own way, managers would only intervene in order to package the outcomes. Artists would enjoy 'autonomy around process', but be kept well away from any strategic thinking beyond their immediate 'creative' role. Fundamentally this approach to cultural management makes an assumption about motivation. According to creativity theorists, most notably Teresa Amabile, creativity is intrinsically motivated – any external interventions will be at best ineffective, at worst distracting or destructive. Consequently, managers stay outside the 'black box' of creativity and at the same time artists are 'buffered' from the organisational and commercial realities around their work.

Chapter 3 addresses Cultural Management 2.0. With a new emphasis on creative industries as an integral part of the future economy, some of the tensions between artists and managers in the 1980s were replaced by an uneasy alliance in the late 1990s. According to the new rhetoric of creativity emanating from DCMS and think tanks like NESTA, managers and creatives were on the same side – both are dealing with unpredictable processes and outcomes, both pursuing 'innovation', both embracing 'entrepreneurial' methods to achieve it (Schlesinger 2007). This chapter centres on entrepreneurial approaches to cultural management, with managers highlighting the importance of individual initiative and capability at the same time as the DCMS was emphasising individual creativity, skill and talent. Thinking opportunistically and flexibly might work for smaller enterprises, but an entrepreneurial approach to cultural management becomes less effective as those enterprises start to grow. Strategic thinking is needed to complement entrepreneurial thinking. Without it, small enterprises follow the boom-bust trajectory of the dot.com years of the late 1990s/early 2000s: explosive unplanned growth driven by ambitious investors; a loss of direction as the core business idea is diluted and the novelty wears off; a collapsing infrastructure as the bubble bursts and investors move on to the next big thing. Cultural Management 2.0 addresses the tension between entrepreneurial and strategic thinking, especially the challenges facing organisations as they grow.

Chapter 4 considers how cultural managers have adapted to the expansion in consumer choice, engagement and creativity made possible by digital technologies. Cultural Management 3.0 is a response to the age of the prosumer (or produser). With cultural consumers increasingly calling the shots and the value of cultural products being redefined through inventive cultural consumption, cultural managers needed to take a more adaptive, responsive approach. The chapter will consider some strategies used by cultural managers to afford greater space for consumer creation – a more vulnerable approach to leadership, accepting the wisdom of the crowd and a more expansive view of where and how cultural value is created. The paradox in this chapter is between leading and following, between producing culture and consuming it.

Chapter 5 is an attempt to gather together these different approaches to management and show how they can be directed towards a single project. 'Leading for Innovation' takes as its starting point the situated nature of leadership (leadership strengths are always dependent on the context of the task, the organisation and the environment) and the multi-stage nature of innovation (beyond the moment of ideation, different stages in the innovation process will require different models of leadership). In the final analysis, the three models of cultural management outlined in this book should be seen as complementary not competing, and each scenario needs to be taken on its merits, requiring a different mix of leadership capabilities.

Notes

1 The UK's Department for Culture, Media and Sport (DCMS) was established by the incoming 'New' Labour government in 1997 as the successor to the previous administrations's Department for National Heritage (known affectionately/dismissively as the 'Department of Fun'). In order to engage with the creative industries, a Creative Industries Task Force was established, supported by industry luminaries from the likes of Virgin and Creation Records. The Task Force consulted with various industry representatives. These consultations would feed into the DCMS Creative Industries Mapping Document (1998, reissued in 2001). This document was very influential not only in the UK but globally in setting out a working definition of the creative industries which politicians could understand and support.

2 Newbigin was one of the report's authors and architects. Speaking at a 2008 seminar on the Creative Industries Ten Years On, Newbigin was rather sceptical of the political and cultural significance which others have attributed to the shift in terminology – or at least, he claimed that these implications were not something he and the other authors of the report had spent much time thinking about at the time. The main aim was to appeal to the politicians by framing the report as something new and exciting.

References

Amabile, T. (1998). How to kill creativity. *Harvard Business Review*, *76*(5), pp. 76–87.

Bennett, T. (1998). Cultural studies: A reluctant discipline. *Cultural Studies*, *12*(4), pp. 528–45.

Bianchini, F. (1987). GLC R.I.P.: Cultural policies in London 1981–1986. *New Formations*, *1* (Spring 1987), pp. 103–17.

Bourdieu, P. (1993). *The Field of Cultural Production: Essays on Art and Literature*. New York: Columbia University Press.

Department for Culture, Media and Sport (1998). *Creative Industries Mapping Document*. London: DCMS.

Deveraux, C. (2018). Cultural management as a field. In: Deveraux, C. (ed.), *Arts and Cultural Management: Sense and Sensibilities in the State of the Field*. New York: Routledge, pp. 3–12.

DiMaggio, P. J. (1986). *Non-Profit Enterprise in the Arts: Studies in Mission and Constraint*. New York: Oxford University Press.

Frank, T. (2001). One market under god: Extreme capitalism. *Market Populism and the End of Economic Democracy*. London: Secker and Warburg.

Garnham, N. (2005). From cultural to creative industries: An analysis of the implications of the "creative industries" approach to arts and media policy making in the United Kingdom. *International Journal of Cultural Policy*, *11*(1), pp. 15–29.

Gitlin, T. (1980). *The Whole World Is Watching: Mass Media in the Making and Unmaking of the New Left*. Berkeley, CA: University of California Press.

Hagoort, G. (2003). *Art Management: Entrepreneurial Style*. Delft: Eburon.

Hall, S., Clarke, J., Jefferson, T. and B. Roberts (1976). Subcultures, cultures and class. In: Hall, S. and Jefferson, T. (eds.), *Resistance Through Rituals: Youth Subcultures in Post-War Britain*. London: Hutchinson, pp. 9–74.

Hebdige, D. (1979): *Subculture: The Meaning of Style*. London: Routledge.

Hills, M. (2002). *Fan Cultures*. London: Routledge.

Hua, F. (2018). Arts and cultural management: A brief, comparative in curricular design: Cases from the UK, USA, and China. In: Deveraux, C. (ed.), *Arts and Cultural Management: Sense and Sensibilities in the State of the Field*. New York: Routledge, pp. 13–38.

Jenkins, H. (2006). *Fans, Bloggers, and Gamers: Exploring Participatory Culture*. New York: New York University Press.

Keat, R. and Abercrombie, N. (eds.) (1991). *Enterprise Culture*. London: Routledge.

Kelly, O. (1984). *Community, Art and the State: Storming the Citadels*. London: Comedia.

Klein, Naomi (2000). *No Logo: Taking Aim at the Brand Bullies*. London: Flamingo.

Koestler, A. (1976). *The Act of Creation*. London: Hutchinson [1964].

Lash, S. and Urry, J. (1994). *Economies of Signs and Space*. London: Sage.

Lee, H. and Lim, L. (eds.) (2014). *Cultural Policies in East Asia: Dynamics between the State, Arts and Creative Industries*. Basingstoke: Palgrave Macmillan.

Mosco, V. (2009). *The Political Economy of Communication* (2nd edition). London: Sage.

Mould, O. (2018). *Against Creativity*. London: Verso Books.

Negus, K. and Pickering, M. (2004). *Creativity, Communication and Cultural Value*. London/Thousand Oaks, CA: Sage.

Oakley, K. (2014). Good work? Rethinking cultural entrepreneurship. In: Bilton, C. and Cummings, S. (eds.), *Handbook of Management and Creativity*. Cheltenham: Edward Elgar, pp. 145–59.

Porter, M. (2001). Strategy and the internet. *Harvard Business Review*, *79*(3) (March 2001), pp. 62–78.

Pratt, A.C. (2005). Cultural industries and public policy: An oxymoron? *International Journal of Cultural Policy*, *11*(1), pp. 31–44.

Pratt, A.C. (2017). Innovation and the cultural economy. In: Batheldt, H., Cohendet, P., Henn, A. and Simon, L. (eds.), *The Elgar Companion to Innovation and Knowledge Creation: A Multi-Disciplinary Approach*. Cheltenham: Edward Elgar, pp. 230–43.

Rosen, J. (2006). The people former known as the audience. *PressThink* 27 June 2006. Available at: http://archive.pressthink.org/2006/06/27/ppl_frmr.html

Schiller, H. (1989). *Culture Inc.–The Corporate Takeover of Public Expression*. New York: Oxford University Press.

Schlesinger, P. (2007) Creativity: From discourse to doctrine? *Screen*, *48*(3), October, pp. 377–87.

Scott, A.J. (1999): The cultural economy: geography and the creative field. *Media, Culture and Society*, *21*, pp. 807–17.

Şuteu, C. (2006). *Another Brick in the Wall: A Critical Review of Cultural Management Education in Europe*. Amsterdam: Boekmanstudies.

Tusa, J. (2003). *On Creativity: Interviews Exploring the Process of Creativity*. London: Methuen publishing.

Throsby, D. (2010). *The Economics of Cultural Policy*. Cambridge: Cambridge University Press.

Williams, R. (1971). Literature and Sociology: In Memory of Lucien Goldmann. *New Left Review*, *67* (May–June 1971), pp. 3–18.

Williams, R. (1977). *Marxism and Literature*. Oxford: Oxford University Press.

Willis, P. (1990). *Common Culture: Symbolic Work at Play in the Everyday Cultures of the Young*. Milton Keynes: Open University Press.

Wright, D. (2018). "Hopeful Work" and the creative economy. In: Martin, L. and Wilson, N. (eds.), *The Palgrave Handbook of Creativity at Work*. Cham: Palgrave Macmillan, pp. 311–25.

Zuboff, S. (2019): *The Age of Surveillance Capitalism: The Fight for a Human Future at the New Frontier of Power*. New York: Public Affairs.

2 Cultural Management 1.0

Managing creativity through freedom and control

Cultural Management 1.0 starts from two assumptions about creativity and management. First of all, creativity is located within the individual, as something mysterious, intuitive and inherently unmanageable. Secondly, management is seen as something external to the creative process, a set of boundaries and controls within which individual creativity can roam but beyond which it cannot stray.

These assumptions reflect the emergence of arts management as an academic discipline and professional practice in the 1980s. As described in Chapter 1, the impetus towards managing artistic organisations and people began in the public sector, with an attempt to make artists and arts organisations more accountable – to funders and to audiences. Given that public subsidy was premised on a rhetoric of widening participation and access to a public good, the failure to deliver on that rhetoric was damaging.

Consequently, the role of the arts manager in the 1980s focused on financial control (avoiding waste and misdirection of public money) and marketing (connecting cultural products to audiences). The creative process which lies behind these inputs and outputs was largely off limits, not least because managers did not claim to understand the arts and artists. As will be discussed later in this chapter, despite often heavy-handed imposition of targets in finance and marketing, there is a humility to Cultural Management 1.0 – it knows its limitations in a way that later iterations perhaps do not.

This chapter will consider some of the assumptions which lie behind these perceptions of cultural management. Whilst they might be rooted in a particular historical moment in the past, some of the stereotypical assumptions about creativity and management (freedom versus control) persist. The chapter will then focus on theories of intrinsic motivation – the idea that creativity is something internal to the creative individual. This idea provides the intellectual basis for Cultural Management 1.0.

DOI: 10.4324/9781003009184-2

Finally, the chapter will consider the value of Cultural Management 1.0 for cultural managers today. Just as there is no single model of 'best practice', so too there can be no universally derided 'worst practice'. There is some value in Cultural Management 1.0, especially in the idea of standing back from the creative process and allowing some aspects of that process to evolve at their own pace.

Freedom and control

A central dilemma in cultural management remains the tension between freedom and control. Stereotypically the creative process is assumed to be unconstrained, autonomous and self-motivated. Management structures around that creative act impose restraints – targets, budgets, deadlines – and these hold the creative process back. This opposition is reinforced through the way organisations are structured, in our education systems, even in the way we speak and dress. Even the old (and discredited) 'hemispheric' theory of 'left brain/right brain' seems to play into the same stereotype – artists use their right brain, they are intuitive, irrational, emotional. Managers are all left brain – deliberate, rational, logical.

Of course this binary opposition is just that – a stereotype. Never mind that creative processes operate within constraints, often self-imposed, which channel and shape the creative outcome. Conversely, management is not only about hierarchy and structure, it can also be geared to opening out channels of thought, building upwards and outwards from individual enterprise rather than bearing down on it.

The opposition between freedom and control reflects a core tenet of creativity theory, the argument that creativity and creative people are internally (intrinsically) motivated. Trying to motivate or influence the creative act from the outside will be at best distracting, at worst destructive. This argument is grounded in empirical research, from psychological experiments to organisational studies.

The other element is more elusive, a cultural division based on values and ideals rather than any empirical evidence. A cluster of beliefs about creative individuals, summarised by Robert Weisberg as 'the myth of genius', is rooted in a longer history, from the humanist ideals of the Renaissance through to the Romanticism of the nineteenth century. Meanwhile, management history has emphasised the scientific, rational nature of management – from Weber's iron cage to Taylor's scientific management. Management historians dispute some of these simplifications – and newer strands of management thought have sought to articulate a more 'creative' approach. We will return to theories of creative management in Chapter 3 in the context of 'Cultural Management 2.0'.

At the time of Cultural Management 1.0 in the 1980s, these stereotypes were in full flow. Management 'discipline' was being imposed on a feckless, irresponsible cultural sector by a government cracking down on waste, demanding accountability and value for money, cutting back on funding and replacing open-ended revenue funding with tightly demarcated project-based funding contracts. Artists, especially those who had cut their teeth during the 1960s counter-culture, railed against a rising tide of corporate control in both the state-funded and commercial cultural sectors, united under the banner of New Managerialism (Power 1999).

My own experience, whilst anecdotal, may reflect some of this zeitgeist. In 1985, I registered our fledgling theatre company with the Enterprise Allowance Scheme, designed to set up the long-term unemployed in business, part of the UK government's attempt to redefine the welfare system, with an emphasis on entrepreneurship, self-help and marketisation. Like many unemployed artists at the time, I had no real interest in business, but the scheme liberated me from the ritual of signing on for benefits while giving me slightly more money in the form of an 'allowance'.

To qualify for the scheme we had to attend mandatory business training. In my case this meant a retired ex-military man in a south London community centre introducing us to the minutiae of petty cash vouchers. If this was what 'management' meant, it clearly bore no relation to the realities of starting a small business, still less one based on a creative practice. In hindsight, some kind of management training would have helped us at the time – instead we sneered our disapproval and convinced ourselves that management was an old man's game. The mismatch between the trainer's version of enterprise management and the experiences of the other people in that community centre encapsulates the cultural differences between 'creatives and suits' which are an integral part of Cultural Management 1.0.

Even though we did not acknowledge the relevance or remit of management training, we still knew that some understanding of finance and marketing might be useful. Nor did our rejection and resistance towards management training undermine our own commitment to a creative career. If anything it made us more entrenched in our belief in the value of our own work and the rightness of our creative decisions – often despite compelling external evidence to the contrary. We attended the training because it was a condition of our funding. But we did not believe in it. That self-belief allowed a handful of businesses to thrive (the fashion label SuperDry famously began life via the Enterprise Allowance Scheme project, trading from a stall in Camden Market), while encouraging many others to crash and burn.

This positioning of management control outside and above the creative process, with artists continuing to 'do our own thing' whilst paying lip service to managerial realities, is at the core of Cultural Management 1.0. As we will consider in the next section, the basis for this separation between creativity and management is embedded in theories of intrinsic motivation. On closer examination the relation between creativity and motivation is more complicated, and the assumption that creativity is self-motivated (and therefore essentially beyond the reach of management control) ignores the different, sometimes contradictory elements which go into the creative process.

Apart from theories of intrinsic motivation, the differences between artists ('creatives') and managers ('suits') are amplified by cultural factors which reinforce mutual suspicion to the point of outright hostility. To some extent these differences are self-serving – granting exemptions from social norms and justifying an introverted mindset on both sides of the divide – but in the end they are dysfunctional and destructive.

The chapter will conclude by considering some of the benefits of Cultural Management 1.0. The emphasis on creativity as irresponsible, individualistic and unmanageable might be a partial, one-sided account – but for certain elements in the creative process it may also be partially accurate. As with most of the binary oppositions considered in this book, in the end the choice between freedom or control is a false one. Creative processes, and management processes, combine freedom *and* control – the challenge is knowing when to intervene and when to step back.

Intrinsic motivation

Any discussion of motivation and creativity must begin with Teresa Amabile's career-spanning investigations of intrinsic motivation and the creative process. With a background in psychology and organisational studies, Amabile's research has included psychological experiments involving heuristic, creative tasks, and studies of organisational behaviour and the ways individual creative capacity is shaped by the organisational environment (Amabile 1988; Amabile and Gryskiewicz 1989; Amabile 1993, 1997, 1998).

Amabile's three-part model of creativity argues that creativity requires three components: domain-specific expertise (craft, technical skills and knowledge within a specific domain), creative thinking skills (cognitive style, ability to generate novel ideas) and task motivation (a sense of fulfilment from completing the creative task) (Amabile 1988, 1997). Many of these elements can be taught or improved through practice – so everybody has the potential to be creative, or to become more creative. The one unmoving fixed component is task motivation – without that fundamental desire to immerse oneself in the creative process, the other components become irrelevant. Organisations and mentors can try to nurture that inner drive, but they cannot create it.

Through much of Amabile's work it seems that the external environment is more likely to hinder than help task motivation. From her childhood experience of a teacher telling her she could not draw to the clumsy attempts from organisations to micro-manage creative individuals, external interventions tend to discourage rather than encourage the creative process. In experimental settings, extrinsic motivations, the carrot and the stick, are no replacement for intrinsic motivation. External rewards might in certain circumstances prove complementary to intrinsic motivation, but more often they undermine the focus on task motivation. External threats (e.g. the threat of external judgement) are almost always negative influences on the creative process. In order to preserve task motivation intact, the best way to manage environmental pressures on the creative process is to minimise them.

This is borne out by studies of work motivation in other areas, especially voluntary work or altruistic behaviour such as donating blood. In these circumstances, where the main drive comes from an internal sense of morality or idealism rather than any external obligation, extrinsic rewards can 'crowd out' intrinsic motivation (Gagné and Deci 2005, 332; Upton 1974). Abraham Maslow described creativity in 1954 as 'unmotivated behaviour' – something that is part of our being, not something that we need. He further argued that creativity is above all an attitude of mind – an openness to uncertainty and unprecedented experiences, 'an affinity for the unknown' (Maslow 1987, 161) and argued that creativity was not restricted to the arts and 'that a first-rate soup is more creative than a second-rate painting, and that generally cooking or parenthood or making a home could be creative while poetry need not be: It could be uncreative' (Maslow 1987, 159). By placing creativity in the category of 'being' rather than 'doing', Maslow reinforces the idea that creativity is unlikely to respond to any external interventions.

The idea that creativity is a positive, rewarding experience is integral to Csikszentmihalyi's notion of 'flow' in which 'a person's skills are fully involved in overcoming a challenge that is just about manageable … in moments which stand out as the best in their lives' (Csikszentmihalyi

1997, 30–2). Csikszentmihalyi was associated with positive psychology and the science of happiness. Creative work continues to be associated with 'good' work – autonomous, self-fulfilling, unconstrained (Banks and Hesmondhalgh 2009, 417). Of course if creativity is its own reward, the free and freely given labour of the creative worker (especially the young creative worker) is ripe for exploitation by others who see this as a source of profit rather than pleasure (McRobbie 2016; Ross 2009).

This is not to say that management of the creative process is impossible or irrelevant – but there needs to be a distance between the individual creative process and the organisational processes around them (Amabile 1998). Maintaining this distance becomes the task of creative or cultural management.

All of this might be true if we restrict our definition of creativity to the generation of new ideas – and in many business settings, this is indeed the primary function of creative or innovative teams and divisions. However, if we are interested in creativity in a cultural setting, we need to acknowledge the multiplicity of the creative process. Ideas are not just being generated, they are being developed, adapted, tested, combined, redirected in a continuing, iterative, cyclical process. Certainly some stages in the process fit with Amabile's description of heuristic, self-motivated thinking – but other stages are more pragmatic and deliberate. Marylène Gagné and Edward Deci describe an 'autonomy continuum' (Gagné and Deci 2005 334–6) with different types of motivation applying to different tasks. Both Baer et al. (2003) and Dew (2009) draw a distinction between 'innovative' and 'adaptive' behaviours – each necessary to the creative process according to Kirton's model (Kirton 1984), but each requiring different types of motivation. Accordingly intrinsic motivation 'waxes and wanes' through the process (Dew 2009). There is also the possibility that extrinsic motivations become internalised and vice versa (Gagné and Deci 2005). There is not always a clear-cut distinction between an innate desire to do the job well, the approval of one's peers and external measures of success including financial success; each of these might be a proxy for the other (Yoon et al 2015).

Part of the problem with research into creativity and motivation is the unit of analysis. In most of the psychological experiments, and in many of the organisational studies, the creativity task will be a self-contained challenge, for example, coming up with a number of new uses for a familiar object like a paperclip. These kinds of heuristic challenges very often stimulate a desire to complete the task as an end in itself. However, by disconnecting the task from its context, the experiment loses any broader understanding of the task's purpose, value and assessment criteria. There is circular logic in using self-contained and inherently satisfying tasks as evidence of 'task fulfilment' (Gagné and Deci 2005, 333).

In other words, the idea that creative thinking is intrinsically motivated is only partly true. Some parts of the process are undoubtedly rewarding and fulfilling. Others are more mundane, even boring. In his discussion of motivation and creativity, Maslow argued that creativity integrates two different kinds of thinking – a primary level of improvisation and spontaneity, and a secondary level involving 'hard work, long training, unrelenting criticism, perfectionistic standards'. It is only when both these components are combined 'or in good succession' that 'integrated creativity' is possible, giving rise to 'the great work of art or philosophy of science' (Maslow 1987 165–6). Task fulfilment might deliver primary-level creative thinking but an immersion in the task might prevent the kind of critical, laborious work required for secondary-level creativity.

Maslow's description of the 'self-actualizing creative' who can integrate 'clashing colors, forms that fight each other, dissonances of all kind, into a unity' (Maslow 1987, 161–2) resonates with Arthur Koestler's theory of bisociation. Intrinsic and extrinsic motivations, as Amabile intimated, can pull the creative process in opposite directions. For Maslow, integrated creativity – the ability 'to put separate and even opposites together into unity' even has a moral dimension:

> To the extent that creativeness is constructive, synthesizing, unifying, and integrative, to that extent does it depend in part on the inner integration of the person.
>
> (Maslow 1987, 162)

Recognising that different people, processes and stages within a process require different kinds of motivation and management is a theme to which we will return in Chapter 5. Meanwhile, treating creativity and creative workers as idealised post-capitalist workers, forever flowing and fulfilled, is clearly an oversimplification. Yet this archetype fits with a certain mythology of creative processes and people.

The myth of genius

Understanding the culture of cultural management means reading behind the lines of methods and models to examine implicit attitudes and language. The emphasis on 'talent' in UK cultural policy, Maslow's description of creativity as 'being' not doing and the intrinsic motivation of the creative process identified by Amabile exemplify the 'culture' of Cultural Management 1.0. Taken together, the cluster of attitudes reviewed in this chapter so far suggest creativity is essentially a personality trait. Talent is not something earned or cultivated; it exists as a gift (occasionally a curse) bestowed on the individual. As such it is not something which can be taught or managed – it is engrained and immutable.

Robert Weisberg began writing about the 'myth of genius' in the 1980s (Weisberg 1986, 1993, 2010). He noted that the idea of the creative individual as a special type of person relied upon the definition of creativity as a special type of thinking. This was contradicted by the importance of multiple types of thinking in the creative process – in particular the importance of technical skill or craft – and the combination of divergent *and* convergent thinking needed to turn initial inspiration into a creative outcome. Intrinsic motivation was important, but as Amabile noted in her componential model of creativity, it was only part of the answer. 'Talent' is nothing without 'skill', associated by Weisberg with domain-specific expertise – a familiarity with the craft and traditions of a particular domain (Banks 2010). Weisberg's critique of the genius myth drew not only on this model of cognition, but also on an understanding of social context. Weisberg showed how a creative individual like Picasso had drawn on traditions (including African art) and on the collective culture of an artistic movement. Memory, shared knowledge and understanding, tradition and craft skills were part of a collective culture. This more systematic understanding of creativity echoed with what has become the dominant paradigm in creativity research, the study of systems and social structures around the creative process in place of a purely cognitive approach (Becker 1982; Sawyer 2006; Woolf 1993; Csikszentmihalyi 1997).

The myth of genius is itself embedded in a culture. Pre-modern cultures tended to equate creativity with the power of the gods. Artists were shamans and God or gods spoke through them, human creativity being an imitation of divine creativity which created the world. Renaissance humanism shifted the attention away from God to man. The first modern geniuses were those Renaissance artists who could not only paint frescoes and ceilings in churches but also portray their wealthy patrons and tell secular stories. These artists could themselves be God-like, not just God-fearing (Negus and Pickering 2004).

During the Romantic era too, artistic genius had a divine, spiritual dimension, from Edmund Burke's concept of the sublime in art to Shelley's defence of poets as the unacknowledged legislators of mankind. Artists and poets, according to Wordsworth, Coleridge and Shelley, represented an alternative to the secular industrial age. That separation of 'art' from industry positions artistic creativity as something free and transcendent, rising above the realities of everyday living to represent what Matthew Arnold called 'the best that has been said and thought in the world'. At the same time, that same separation between art and industry cuts artistic creativity off from reality, driving an exquisitely crafted wedge between aesthetic culture and the everyday tasks of living. Following William Morris's critique of the separation of art from useful work, we also hear in the late nineteenth century the first rumblings of the 'uselessness' of art, its irrelevance and disconnection from ordinary living and ordinary people, and attempts to reconnect creative genius with the older idea of 'genius' representing the spirit of a place, a shared understanding. This is the story told by Raymond Williams in *Culture and Society* – the separation and reconciliation between idealist and materialist theories of art and culture (Williams 1990).

Romantic theories of art form part of the culture of Cultural Management 1.0. If the myth of genius reinforces the idea of creative individuals as unaccountable and unmanageable, Romanticism proposes that creativity, especially artistic creativity, is the opposite of commerce. The artist must answer a higher calling than material living. He (and the artist, like the genius, was usually gendered as male) stands outside and in opposition to materialism, commerce and mediocrity. To impose managerial constraints on artistic creativity is to destroy its essence. Romanticism has continued to inform attitudes to cultural management in our own century (Lee 2005), in particular that creative processes and people should be protected from management intervention.

Whilst discredited in academia and difficult to sustain in an increasingly collaborative, collective creative sector, the myth of genius still carries some weight. One possible reason for this might be the search for certainty in a complex and uncertain industry. Unpredictability cuts through all of the models of cultural management considered in this book, from the risky entrepreneurial business models in Cultural Management 2.0. to postmodern theories of value and identity influencing Cultural Management 3.0. Cultural Management 1.0 addresses the central problem of unpredictable incomes and outputs by relating uncertainty to individual agency.

In the film industry, Thorsten Hennig-Thurau (Hennig-Thurau and Houston 2019) has described the 'nobody knows anything trap'. 'Nobody knows anything' was the famous phrase used by screenwriter William Goldman in *Adventures in the Screen Trade* to describe the extreme uncertainty governing decisions in the film industry. The problem with such a mentality, according to Hennig-Thurau and

Houston, is firstly that it ignores the importance of data analytics in making smart decisions on approving, budgeting and marketing in the film industry – if somebody makes a mistake, 'nobody knows anything' and no lessons are learned. The other problem is that it invests great power and trust in individual decision-makers – extending the myth of genius to a mythology of heroic leadership (Bilton 2010; Prichard 2002; Nisbett and Walmsley 2016).

'Nobody knows anything' invests power in a handful of senior executives who are given absolute power over decisions with no real accountability – by the time that failure emerges, the executive in charge has moved on to the next project, and blame can be shuffled on to a range of unpredictable factors outside his control. An aura of invincibility is constructed around the Hollywood mogul – if nobody knows anything, those who can find gold in the dirt are accorded a mythical, mystical status. This myth of God-like genius helps to build a momentum around each project, drawing others into their orbit and escalating decisions by others who are persuaded to commit resources, talent and time. The consecration by the genius producer thus becomes almost self-fulfilling, a result of cascading decisions and belief which is difficult to reverse. And because this effect is useful to the film company, the myth that this is all down to the genius of one man is maintained – even if that man has some personal flaws, it is better not to look too closely. This is the goose laying the golden eggs.

There are examples of this in many sectors – the sanctification of Steve Jobs at Apple, the TED talks praising Pixar executives. In many cases the heroic leader is given a free pass by followers when faced with allegations of bullying or harassment. More mundanely, the myth of the heroic leader allows senior managers to eke out a reputation across an entire career: the ex-A&R man who once signed a successful band, the advertising executive who once presided over a ground-breaking creative campaign. In his research into K-pop leaders, Dongjoon Lee has shown how the myth of the creative genius and the myth of the heroic leader come together in the person of 'artist-leaders'. Producers like S M Lee and J Y Park have used their artistic reputation to build a reputation as visionary, heroic leaders (Lee 2021).

The most egregious exemplar of this 'heroic' decision-making culture was Harvey Weinstein, the disgraced producer once considered a genius by those around him and memorably described by Meryl Streep as 'God'. Weinstein rightly ended his career in ignominy and disgrace, but the culture which enabled him has proved more resilient. The #MeToo movement could be evidence of a new culture of zero tolerance towards sexual exploitation – but it has continued to pick off individuals rather than tackling a culture. So long as the film industry believes that success and failure are down to the decisions of a powerful individual, 'nobody knows anything' provides an alibi for all kinds of misconduct and exploitation. Because the individual genius is so precious to the industry, they are exempted from the normal rules of behaviour. Those around them will enable their transgressions and cover them up when accusers come forward.

Weinstein shows us the toxic side of genius, the 'talented' individual whose gift is unexplainable and unaccountable. His career also reminds us how 'genius' privileges a certain type of person and way of thinking, and normalises behaviours which would otherwise be unacceptable. For Weinstein these behaviours centred around toxic masculinity and gender inequality, but the very idea of special people with special abilities reinforces other inequalities too especially ethnicity and class differences – and the creative industries continue to be more unequal and more exploitative than many other sectors, not least because many still believe that unquantifiable 'talent' is more important than measurable 'skill'.

Since this is a book about cultural management, the other important negative effect of the myth of genius is organisational. The perceived difference between the genius and the non-genius, the visionary and the enabler, the innovator and the adapter, the creative and the suit reinforce dysfunctional divisions in organisations. These divisions are further bolstered by educational specialisations (especially in the UK), by gender (the male genius and the female factotum), by culture (dress codes, language, cultural capital). The hierarchy applies both to creative individuals and to visionary leaders, separated out from the supporting cast of unheroic creative workers who turn their ideas into realities.

To some extent Cultural Management 1.0 reinforces these divisions, removing or 'buffering' the creative individual from organisational realities, and removing management from the creative process. This not only diminishes and infantilises the creative process, it also reduces cultural management (apart from the heroic leader) to bureaucratic administration, something involving petty cash vouchers and paperwork.

One paradoxical outcome of cultural management was to build a mythology around both the creative individual and the heroic leader, privileging but also polarising them to the point where they no longer engage with each other. Reconnecting these perspectives, reining in the extremes and rebuilding the missing middle where much of the real work takes place would be a major impetus for Cultural Management 2.0.

Whilst all of these criticisms and more can be directed at Cultural Management 1.0, there is nevertheless something worth saving here. In the final part of this chapter, I will consider the benefits of Cultural Management 1.0.

Cultural Management 1.0: a partial solution

This chapter has considered Cultural Management 1.0 as the binary opposition between management control and creative 'freedom'. This opposition is rooted in stereotypical assumptions about the nature of creativity and the nature of management, in particular cultural attitudes to creative people and processes (the myth of genius). It also assumes that creative people and processes are intrinsically motivated, thereby limiting the effectiveness of management interventions.

A large part of cultural management then becomes a matter of human resources – identify, recruit and retain the best creative people, then let them get on with their work with as little interference as possible. This HR approach to creativity is supported by the use of personality tests such as Myers Briggs Type Index to separate the creative from the uncreative.

When it comes to the creative process itself, Cultural Management 1.0 adopts a laissez-faire approach. Because management intervention is likely to crowd out intrinsic motivation and interrupt creative flow, non-intervention becomes a strategy in its own right. By protecting the creative process from external interference, removing or deferring external constraints, managers will allow creativity to flourish. The manager's task is peripheral to the creative process, only stepping in once the creative outcome is achieved – at this point the manager can position and market the product.

An arts marketing book published in 1994 (three years before the 1997 watershed which ushered in Cultural Management 2.0) encapsulates this hands-off approach to the creative process:

> The primary aim of arts marketing is to bring an appropriate number of people, drawn from the widest possible social background, economic condition and age, into an appropriate form of contact with the artist, and in so doing to arrive at the best financial outcome that is compatible with the achievement of that aim.
>
> (Diggle 1994, 25)

Reflecting on this definition of 'arts marketing', François Colbert notes the distinction between 'commercial' and 'artistic' enterprises:

> Unlike the commercial sector, which creates a product according to consumer needs, artistic concerns create a product first and then try to find the appropriate clientele.
>
> (Colbert 2007, 11)

What is striking here is the protection of the integrity of the artistic process. To introduce commercial concerns before the product is created would limit artistic freedom and compromise the work's integrity. In Diggle's definition, artistic work should be available to all, not targeted according to a marketing strategy, so the marketer's job is limited to something more like promotion than strategic marketing – and there is certainly no question of the arts marketer advising the artist on the direction of their work.

As noted above, this division is somewhat artificial – should the artist not care about the audience and reception of their work? By excluding artists from these commercial decisions, managers treat them as unruly children, insulated from the serious business of the organisation. Something similar used to happen in advertising agencies where creative teams were kept away from clients in the 1980s and 1990s, partly to protect the client from irresponsible outbursts but also to afford maximum freedom to the creative team. This practice of 'buffering' creative work is less common in today's advertising industry but reflects the divisive logic of Cultural Management 1.0. In the end, the creative process is not just kept at arm's length from commercial realities, it is also kept in the dark. With incomplete information, the creative team might be misdirecting its efforts, wasting energy on unproductive exploration, and missing out on the external challenges and opportunities which could trigger new creative solutions. The dysfunctional separation between 'creatives' and 'suits' is a reflection of the ways in which advertising agencies were structured, with hierarchical and functional divisions and specialisations leading to mutual wariness if not outright hostility (Nixon 2003; Pratt 2006).

These criticisms of Cultural Management 1.0 are only partially justified. Many artists reading these pages might find themselves nodding in agreement with Keith Diggle, and wishing they could be a bit more 'buffered' from managerial interventions and commercial realities. As previously discussed, intrinsic motivation, immersion and fulfilment in the creative tasks provide the theoretical basis for Cultural Management 1.0. But intrinsic motivation 'waxes and wanes' across different stages in the creative process (Dew 2009, 946). Some parts of the process, especially the early heuristic stages of search and discovery, are more intrinsically motivated and might indeed benefit from a light touch approach

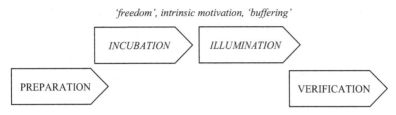

Figure 2.1 Motivation in the creative process.

to management. Other stages – the pre-ideation phase of preparation and planning, the later stages of application, development and product-testing might benefit from a more interventionist management style. In Wallas's classic four-stage model of the creative process we could identify alternating phases of freedom and control through the creative process (Figure 2.1).

The idea of interchanging between freedom and control lies behind Tom Peters' formulation of organisations which are 'simultaneously loose and tight'(Peters and Waterman 2004), but in a cultural context is perhaps best summarised by Amabile's call for 'autonomy around process' (Amabile 1998). Amabile argued for strategic clarity around intended outcomes and operational flexibility around methods. This points to a more positive version of Cultural Management 1.0. There is a degree of predictability and familiarity in the separation of roles, between the creative and the managerial, which allows managers to manage and creatives to create. Autonomy around process acknowledges the intrinsically motivated nature of some parts of the creative process and warns against micro-management. By stepping back from the process, managers allow some space and time for unpredictable creative processes to play out – especially during the 'incubation' phase of creativity, where potential ideas and solutions are allowed to percolate and exchange prior to the breakthrough of 'illumination'. As Figure 2.1 indicates above, in these phases of the creative process, freedom and autonomy for the artist require non-intervention from the manager.

For all its faults then, Cultural Management 1.0 has its merits – for certain types of process, certain types of people, certain types of task. At times the best action for the manager is not to act – to let actions and decisions unfold at their own pace. It is notable too that Cultural Management 1.0 often refers to 'the arts' – as in arts management and arts marketing. Early arts management texts prefer the more modest 'administration' over the more domineering connotations of 'management'. John Pick's pioneering work, *Arts Administration* (Pick and Anderton 1996), represents peak Cultural Management 1.0 – originally published in 1980 with a second edition in 1996, the book drew on Pick's experience as leader of one of the first 'arts management' courses in the UK (and indeed in the world) established at City University in 1976. Throughout the book, Pick is impatient with management jargon, especially the 'bureaucracy' of targets, performance indicators and other 'extrinsic goals' imposed by governments and funding bodies, and calls for 'vigilance' from arts administrators to protect the integrity of the 'aesthetic contract' from managerial overreach. Pick memorably referred to the Arts Council of Great Britain as 'vile jelly' and maintained a simmering resentment towards 'bureaucrats', not least because they sought to intervene in the aesthetic contract between artist and audience. Like Diggle, Pick assumed that the role of the arts administrator was as a matchmaker – not intervening in the artistic process but connecting the artistic product to its 'proper' audience in order to maximise its aesthetic effect, not its financial return.

Whilst Pick occasionally references popular music, publishing, television or Disney theme parks, the main thrust of his argument is directed at publicly funded arts organisations. Twenty years later, with the shift from arts to cultural or creative industries in the late 1990s, the relationship between creativity and management and the centrality of the Arts Council in that relationship has surely changed. But Pick's idea of protecting artists from interfering bureaucracy still remains relevant, especially in the subsidised sector. The same could be said of Cultural Management 1.0 – it is not a comprehensive system, but it can offer a partial solution to some aspects of cultural management.

The other element worth highlighting in Cultural Management 1.0 is the attempt to treat artists and creators empathetically and holistically. Instead of conventional transactional or transformational leadership strategies, Cultural Management 1.0 attempts to treat the creative person as a unique individual. Without intervening in the creative process, Cultural Management 1.0 nevertheless manifests in 'supportive behaviour' which in turn requires 'emotional intelligence' (Zhou and George 2003). The emotional, irrational side of the creative process is given due recognition (perhaps a little too much), not least because this fits with the stereotype of an unmanageable artist. Again, this might not be the whole answer when managing a creative process or team, but empathy and emotional intelligence (EQ) might still be useful tools to apply in some scenarios.

We can conclude this chapter by conceding that Cultural Management 1.0 remains relevant, especially to certain stages in the creative process and certain types of cultural organisation. It may also have value for certain artistic temperaments, especially those who, like Pick, bristle at interference from incompetent outsiders. Yet it also imposes divisions and stereotypical roles on cultural organisations and workers, it ignores the synergies between commercial and creative objectives and it consecrates art and artists as both unmanageable and irreproachable. Something different was needed as the line between commercial culture and subsidised arts became increasingly blurred, and artists began to manage themselves as independent cultural entrepreneurs, as began to occur in the late 1990s with the ascendance of commercial creative and media industries. Cultural Management 2.0 emerged from this new cultural context – bringing with it a fresh set of paradoxes and contradictions.

References

Amabile, T. (1988). A model of creativity and innovation in organizations. *Research in Organizational Behavior*, *10*(1), pp. 123–67.

Amabile, T. (1993). Motivational synergy: Toward new conceptualizations of intrinsic and extrinsic motivation in the workplace. *Human Resource Management Review*, *3*(3), pp. 185–201.

Amabile, T. (1997) Motivating creativity in organizations: On doing what you love and loving what you do. *California Management Review*, *40*(1), pp. 39–58.

Amabile, T. (1998). How to kill creativity. *Harvard Business Review*, *76*(5), pp. 76–87.

Amabile, T. and Gryskiewicz, N. (1989). The creative environment scales: Work environment inventory. *Creativity Research Journal*, *2*(4), pp. 231–253.

Baer, M., Oldham, G.R. and Cummings, A. (2003). Rewarding creativity: When does it really matter? *The Leadership Quarterly*, *14*(4/5), pp. 569–86.

Banks, M. (2010). Craft labour and creative industries. *International Journal of Cultural Policy*, *16*(3), pp. 305–21.

Banks, M. and Hesmondhalgh, D. (2009). Looking for work in creative industries policy. *International Journal of Cultural Policy*, *15*(4), pp. 415–30.

Becker, H. (1982). *Art Worlds*. Los Angeles: UCLA Press.

Bilton, C. (2010). Manageable creativity. *International Journal of Cultural Policy*, *16*(3), pp. 255–69.

Colbert, F. (2007). *Marketing Culture and the Arts* (3rd edition). Montreal: HEC Montreal.

Csikszentmihalyi, M. (1997). *Finding Flow*. New York: Basic Books.

Dew, R. (2009). Creative resolve response: How changes in creative motivation relate to cognitive style. *The Journal of Management Development*, *28*(10), pp. 945–66.

Diggle, K. (1994). *Arts Marketing*. London: Rheingold.

Gagné, M. and Deci, E.L. (2005). Self-determination theory and work motivation. *Journal of Organizational Behavior*, *26*(4), pp. 331–62.

Hennig-Thurau, T. and Houston, M.B. (2019). *Entertainment Science. Data Analytics and Practical Theory for Movies, Games, Books, and Music*. Cham: Springer.

Kirton, M.J. (1984). Adapters and innovators – Why new initiatives get blocked. *Long Range Planning*, *17*(2), pp. 137–43.

Lee, D. (2021). *Strategic Organisational Change and Artist-Leadership in the K-Pop Industry: A Narrative Analysis Approach* (Doctoral dissertation, University of Warwick).

Lee, H-K. (2005). When arts met marketing: Arts marketing theory embedded in romanticism. *International Journal of Cultural Policy*, *11*(1), 289–305.

Maslow, A. (1987). *Motivation and Personality* (3rd edition). New York: Harper & Row [1954].

McRobbie, A. (2016). *Be Creative: making a living in the new culture industries*. Cambridge: Polity Press.

Negus, K. and Pickering, M. (2004) *Creativity, Communication and Cultural Value*. London/Thousand Oaks, CA: Sage.

Nisbett, M. and Walmsley, B. (2016). The romanticization of charismatic leadership in the arts. *The Journal of Arts Management, Law, and Society*, *46*(1), pp.2–12.

Nixon, S. (2003). *Advertising cultures, gender, commerce, creativity*, London: Sage.

Peters, T. and Waterman, R. (2004). *In Search of Excellence: Lessons from America's Best-Run Companies*. London: Profile Books [1982].

Pick, J. and Anderton, M. (1996) *Arts Administration*. London: E & FN Spon.

Power, M. (1999). *The Audit Society: rituals of verification*. Oxford: Oxford University Press.

Pratt, A. (2006) Advertising and creativity: a governance approach. A case study of creative agencies in London, *Environment and Planning A* 38(10), pp. 1883–1899.

Prichard, C. (2002). 'Creative selves? Critically reading 'creativity' in management discourse. *Creativity and Innovation Management*, *11*(4), pp. 265–76.

Ross, A. (2009). *Nice Work if You Can Get It: Life and Labour in Precarious Times*. New York: New York University Press.

Sawyer, R.K. (2006). *Explaining Creativity*. Oxford: Oxford University Press.

Upton, W.E. (1973) *Altruism, Attribution, and Intrinsic Motivation in the Recruitment of Blood Donors*. Dissertation, Cornell University, 1973.

Weisberg, R.W. (1986). *Creativity: Genius and Other Myths*. New York: W.H. Freeman.

Weisberg, R.W. (1993). *Creativity: Beyond the Myth of Genius*. New York: W.H. Freeman.

Weisberg, R. (2010). The study of creativity: from genius to cognitive science. *International Journal of Cultural Policy*, *16*(3), pp. 235–53.

Williams, R. (1990). *Culture and Society: Coleridge to Orwell* (first published 1958). London: Hogarth Press.

Woolf, J. (1993). *The Social Production of Art*. Basingstoke: Macmillan.

Yoon, H.J., Sung, S.Y., Choi, J.N., Lee, K. and Kim, S. (2015). Tangible and intangible rewards and employee creativity: The mediating role of situational extrinsic motivation. *Creativity Research Journal*, *27*(4), pp. 383–93.

Zhou, J. and George, J.M. (2003). Awakening employee creativity: The role of leader emotional intelligence. *The Leadership Quarterly*, *14*(4/5), pp. 545–68.

3 Cultural Management 2.0

Managing change through cultural entrepreneurship

The election of the UK's New Labour government in 1997 signalled a new emphasis on 'creative industries', underlined in the mapping documents of 1998 and 2001 and in the creation of the Creative Industries Taskforce. In this moment, some of the paradoxes of cultural management were rethought. First, the opposition between creativity and commerce was less applicable in the commercial creative sector – in television, film and popular music, work could be both artistic *and* commercial (Negus 1995). The arm's length distance between autonomous creativity and management control was also shortened – as suggested towards the end of Chapter 2, different stages in the creative process require different motivations and therefore different degrees of management control. In any case, most creative businesses in the commercial sector were smaller and more informally structured with a more fluid relationship between administrative and creative roles. At the same time, 'creativity' was becoming a buzzword in mainstream management theory and practice.

The New Labour government aimed to smooth out some of the controversies and conflicts, which had dogged UK cultural policy towards the creative industries into a new consensus. The attitude to business especially was more relaxed and less critical than in previous Labour administrations. This rapprochement between business and UK political attitudes resonated with the new social democratic centre left taking power in other Western European democracies and with the Clinton administration in the United States. Applying this same pro-business attitude to the cultural sector, the UK government approach was not dissimilar to the famous Andy Warhol quote: 'Being good in business is the most fascinating kind of art. Making money is art and working is art and good business is the best art'. Cultural management books (Bilton 2007; Parrish 2005) highlighted the creative possibilities of management (creative management) and the extent to which

DOI: 10.4324/9781003009184-3

creative processes needed to be directed and targeted (managed creativity). Indeed, 'creativity' became increasingly identified with innovation (including business process innovation) and entrepreneurship. Agencies like National Endowment for Science, Technology and the Arts (NESTA) highlighted these connections between art, technology, innovation and entrepreneurship (Schlesinger 2007), which spilled over into the school curriculum where 'creativity' was no longer limited to the arts (NACCCE 1999; Neelands and Choe 2010).

As management theory and management training adjusted to this new context, attention also shifted away from large, bureaucratic subsidised arts organisations towards smaller, independent creative enterprises. Cultural Management 2.0 was focused on small creative enterprises and individual 'artrepreneurs' capable of both creative and business innovation (Hagoort 2003). Whereas managerialism was framed in opposition to creativity under Cultural Management 1.0, entrepreneurship appeared more aligned with a creative thinking approach.

This chapter considers Cultural Management 2.0 as a form of cultural entrepreneurship – small creative enterprises identifying new products and markets and building economic as well as aesthetic value. Like Cultural Management 1.0 discussed in Chapter 2, this approach solves some problems of cultural management but exposes others.

Each chapter of this book addresses a paradox of cultural management. The central paradox of Cultural Management 2.0 is the tension between short-term opportunism (entrepreneurship) and long-term sustainability (strategy). As the organisation grows, the strengths of an entrepreneurial approach to management become liabilities and a more strategic approach is required to address organisational change. The cultural entrepreneur – celebrated as a maverick outsider and rule-breaker – finds themself in a position of power and responsibility. At this point, the cultural entrepreneur must become a cultural leader. Managing that transition will entail developing some new competences and perspectives.

The digital turn

What I am describing as 'Cultural Management 2.0' is associated with the emergence of digital models of production and consumption – specifically the rise in dotcom businesses from 1999 into the early 2000s. Long before the UK government's DCMS moved from 'Department of Culture, Media and Sport' to 'Digital Culture Media and Sport', UK creative industries policy embraced the emergence of digital creativity on the internet. The inclusion of 'interactive leisure software' (gaming) in the designated list of creative industries was an indicator of government enthusiasm for emerging online businesses, mirroring the interest of investors, especially venture capital, in this sector.

Napster, the music file–sharing service which transformed the music industry, launched in 1999. Around the same time, Google was moving from start-up phase to growth, fuelled by venture capital investors. Facebook followed a similar path a few years later, transforming what had been a campus social network into a public site in 2006. YouTube launched in 2005. American venture capital fuelled their start-up and growth, triggering a feeding frenzy from other investors buying into the 'dot.com' miracle. Online businesses required little in the way of conventional infrastructure and were capable of rapid growth, expanding through the geometric progression of a network rather than the incremental curve of conventional linear growth. Of course, many of these investments failed – not least because investors fuelled unrealistic growth projections – and the dot.com boom inevitably led to a bust. But investors simply transferred their attention to the next big thing. The rhetoric behind these investments focused on start-ups, disruption, new entrants, game-changers, encapsulated in Zuckerberg's mantra 'move fast and break things', and the belief that new technologies gave the competitive edge to start-ups rather than incumbent businesses (Christenson 1997).

In the cultural sector, the digital turn shifted focus from production to distribution and consumption. Digital intermediaries were able to produce more content more cheaply, with less investment in quality control and product development, and then to distribute that content further and over a longer period with very low marginal costs. As a result, digital intermediaries such as Napster and YouTube allowed customers more access and choice than traditional publishers and distributors. Product quality might have been lower but access was higher – allowing individuals to filter the content themselves and find their own diamonds in the dirt. Traditional gatekeepers (broadcasters, record labels, book publishers) had focused on controlling supply, filtering cultural products through a narrowing funnel and relying on a handful of hit products to subsidise uncertain investments in potential products, with a typical success rate of one hit for every ten misses. Digital technologies allowed greater innovation in product delivery (the user experience), not just in product development (the content) – again, this shifted power and focus away from cultural production towards cultural consumption (Hesmondhalgh and Meier 2018).

Digital intermediaries had much lower costs of both distribution and reproduction (the costs of digital reproduction being close to zero) and no longer had to control supply, offering instead an all-you-can-eat digital buffet. The 'disintermediation' of traditional gatekeepers in the new digital economy seemed to signal a new era of abundance, with consumers having direct access to vast swathes of content, instantly and simultaneously, at the click of a mouse. As the new wave of content became a torrent, the tidal wave of entertainment and information threatened to swamp the consumer and drown out originality, quality and authenticity. Disintermediation gave way to reintermediation, with new intermediaries promising to control the flow, aggregating and filtering content, providing new forms of choice and new inventories.

The early 2000s accordingly saw a reconfiguring of the creative industries value chain, with one set of mostly analogue intermediaries being replaced by a new wave of mostly digital services. Crucially, these new digital intermediaries made money not by investing in and profiting from cultural production, but by investing in and profiting from the process of consumption, or more specifically by commodifying consumers themselves. Consequently, broadband providers, digital music services, social networks, retail aggregators were in effect 'content agnostic' – it did not matter to them what was being consumed, so long as the consumer was spending time online consuming. In the attention economy, consumer information was the prize and content was merely the bait.

The consequences of this shift are still with us and will be discussed further in Chapter 4, with the shift to consumer creativity or co-creation. At this stage, it is sufficient to note that during the early 2000s, the value chain of the creative economy moved from analogue to digital, and that the new intermediaries were no longer concerned with the dynamics of cultural production, centring their business model instead on the cultural consumer. At the same time, disruption of traditional value chains opened up new opportunities for entrepreneurial businesses able to adapt to an environment of instability and change. Having greater control and autonomy over content came with a cost – it continues to be very hard to survive as a content creator in this new environment, and the economics of streaming digital content compare very unfavourably with the traditional publishing model in music, books or film. Nevertheless, these entrepreneurial creative businesses set the tone for Cultural Management 2.0.

Whereas Cultural Management 1.0 was wedded to a romantic faith in the transcendent power of great art, Cultural Management 2.0 was more pragmatic and adaptive. Like the big tech companies that broke open the creative industries value chain, the new generation of cultural entrepreneurs were alert to changing patterns of cultural consumption and prepared to remake cultural production around the needs of the consumer rather than the other way around. Speed, flexibility and task completion replaced the patient nurturing of talent and the drag of aesthetic idealism. If all of this sounds like an implied criticism, it's important to acknowledge that the creative industries were ripe for a new managerial approach, and Cultural Management 2.0 offers some valuable alternatives to the limitations of Cultural Management 1.0.

Creative business, creativity in business?

Canadian Henry Mintzberg has been a prominent critic of Anglo-American business schools and the assumptions about management they represent. A principal thrust of this criticism has been the association of top-down business planning – part of the ethos of Cultural Management 1.0 reviewed in Chapter 2– with the hierarchical structures of Anglo-American multi-divisional corporations in the post-1945 period.

In his critique of strategic planning (Mintzberg 1994), Mintzberg raised a number of objections to this approach, which he argued is outdated when dealing with the more unpredictable, discontinuous changes facing today's businesses – especially in the creative industries. Furthermore, echoing Douglas McGregor's 'Theory X and Theory Y' (McGregor 1960) and theories of motivation reviewed in Chapter 2, Mintzberg argued that predetermined top-down strategy restricts individual autonomy, initiative and risk-taking. Theory X rewards compliance, providing no incentive to go beyond prescribed targets or expectations; Theory Y attempts to mobilise intrinsic motivation, encouraging workers to take ownership of their work and rewarding the surprising and the creative, not the predictable and pre-planned. Mintzberg argued that conforming to a top-down 'plan' may get in the way of 'planning' and active engagement from below, especially on the operational frontline. To put it more bluntly, deliberate top-down planning is the enemy of creativity.

Mintzberg's alternative to this was what he called 'emergent strategy' (Mintzberg and Waters 1985). Emergent strategy is a bottom-up process, reacting to opportunities and initiatives on the ground rather than attempting to predict and pre-empt the outcomes in advance. This more contingent approach to strategy places greater trust in the abilities of frontline workers to adapt, invent and respond flexibly to unpredicted (and unpredictable) events. Crucially, it allows more scope for entrepreneurial risk-taking and creativity.

Mintzberg's work resonated with the emerging realities of the digital creative economy, with the dot.com start-ups improvising without a clear plan, often outflanking traditional hierarchical corporations, adapting to rapid and unpredictable technological changes. It also seemed to fit with the ways many creative businesses have tended to operate because, as noted in Chapter 1 of this book, 'symbolic goods' are inherently unpredictable both in the production process and in the response from consumers. One of Mintzberg's earliest case studies of 'emergent strategy' in practice was based on a longitudinal study of a creative organisation, the National Film Board of Canada (Mintzberg and McHugh 1985).

Following on from Mintzberg's pioneering work on strategy formation, other management theorists began to place greater emphasis on 'creativity' in business. Management academics looked to the film industry as an alternative model for organisational processes and decision-making (DeFillippi and Arthur 1998; Lampel, Lant and Shamsie 2000). Jazz, for example, emerged as a popular managerial metaphor to describe the resilience and improvisation needed by 21st-century businesses in place of prediction and planning (Barrett 1988; Hatch 1998, 1999; Weick 1998). Mintzberg himself compared business leadership to conducting an orchestra (Mintzberg 1998; Wallin 2006). More anecdotally, terms like 'creative business' and 'creative management' became increasingly popular. A Google Ngram search shows the usage of 'creative business' rising steadily from 1980 to 2013 and the usage of 'creative management' follows a similar trajectory, peaking in 1988. This needs to be seen in the context of 'creativity' itself becoming an increasingly popular term, to the point where overuse may have diluted its meaning into an empty slogan:

> 'Creative', 'creation', 'creativity' are some of the most overused and ultimately debased words in the language. Stripped of any special significance by a generation of bureaucrats, civil servants, managers and politicians, lazily used as political margarine to spread approvingly and inclusively over any activity with a non-material element to it, the word 'creative' has become almost become unusable
> (Tusa 2003, 5–6)

Certainly, 'creativity' in the mind of a management theorist might not mean quite the same thing as it does for a musician (Prichard 2002). Practically speaking, the rhetoric of freedom and autonomy does not square with the lived experience of content creators, struggling to survive at the bottom of the industry food chain. Nevertheless, as we approached the millennium, the yoking together of creativity and business represented a major shift from Cultural Management 1.0.

Where Cultural Management 1.0 sees creativity and management as opposites, to be kept as far apart from one another as possible, Cultural Management 2.0 sees them as inseparable and overlapping, two sides of the same flexible, improvisatory, unpredictable coin.

Entrepreneurial thinking

These lines of development – the fast-growing (and fast-failing) digital economy, a new faith in 'creativity' as an alternative basis for 'management' and a creative industries policy focused on small, independent businesses – converged on the idea of cultural entrepreneurship (Ellmeier 2003; Naudin 2017).

Cultural entrepreneurship, like cultural management, is a paradoxical blending of capitalistic means and sociocultural ends. The key to cultural entrepreneurship is the social, economic and political shift in the 2000s towards individual agency rather than relying on corporate and state structures to support enterprise, change and individual self-fulfilment. The rise of enterprise culture is associated with the outsourcing of risk from the collective to the individual (Beck 1992), an expectation that creative individuals will find personal fulfilment and financial security if they take the initiative themselves (McRobbie 2015), even if many cultural entrepreneurs act out of necessity rather than choice, as the only path open to them if they are seeking a creative career (Oakley 2014; McRobbie 2002). Oakley, McRobbie and Beck are all quite sceptical about the promise of cultural entrepreneurship as the key to fulfilling, autonomous happy lives. Mostly, the promises have not been kept, and many cultural entrepreneurs (especially young people) find themselves pursuing the dream of 'good work' whilst living the reality of self-exploitation and deferred gratification (Wright 2018).

From a cultural management perspective, cultural entrepreneurship (and by extension, Cultural Management 2.0) has three related characteristics:

- Opportunistic, adaptive approach to decision-making
- Engaging with distribution as well as production
- Emphasis on individual agency, alongside reliance on shared networks

Entrepreneurial decision-making

The cultural entrepreneur's approach to decision-making picks up on Mintzberg's challenge to strategic planning. Rather than trying to plan and pre-empt uncertainty by predicting and controlling the future, entrepreneurs accept uncertainty as inevitable and adapt to whatever they find there. In other words, cultural entrepreneurs act first and plan later. The entrepreneurial mindset is 'ready-fire-aim' – this being similar to Mintzberg's model of emergent strategy, where strategic patterns emerge from a stream of operational decisions not from a cabal of senior managers (Mintzberg and Waters 1985). Saras Sarasvathy (2001) describes this as 'effectual reasoning' as opposed to 'causal reasoning'. Whereas a conventional business might begin with a set of objectives and arrange its resources and actions to pursue a strategic goal (starting with the 'cause' or purpose), an entrepreneur is more likely to start with resources and actions and follow wherever these take it (adapting to the 'effect'). For this reason, entrepreneurs are better able to adapt to unexpected, discontinuous change – partly because they typically have less to lose than a larger corporate organisation accountable to existing stakeholders and customers (Christenson 1997; Stevenson 1983). They are also more likely to trust in their own instincts and judgements.

'Agile' methodology is an approach to project management developed in the software industry, which reflects many of these entrepreneurial principles. Rather than pursuing fixed objectives, the agile team will set daily tasks and allow the longer term objectives to emerge from continuous action. The 'agile manifesto' emphasises the importance of trusting individuals, allowing teams to adapt and self-tune rather than following set protocols and 'responding to change over following a plan' (https://agilemanifesto.org).

Schumpeter (1939) emphasised that the macroeconomic function of the entrepreneur is to open up new markets and discover new products. Entrepreneurs are able to do this precisely because they are not tied to existing products and markets, and they are not locked into a formal process of strategic planning. That more deliberate approach to decision-making would delay action to the point where many opportunities would either have passed or been claimed by a more agile, entrepreneurial competitor.

Considering the social context of the early 2000s, this entrepreneurial approach to decision-making fitted with a perception of changing times, especially rapid changes brought about by digital technology in the cultural and media sector. The attitude to risk – try now, think later, jump first then worry about landing – reflects the influence of venture capital as a source of funding for many entrepreneurial ventures, especially online. Creative and media enterprises had always found it difficult to raise capital from conventional lenders including banks because they were seen to be high risk. Venture capitalists were happy to take a risk if they could also identify a high return. Cultural entrepreneurs satisfied the criterion of high risk; high return was more contentious because most cultural enterprises remained relatively small scale in terms of turnover and employees. Consequently, venture capital fuelled a reckless pursuit of growth and encouraged the casino economics of boom and bust which left a high proportion of failures in pursuit of a few successful 'unicorns'. With or without venture capital, cultural entrepreneurs in the 2000s were caught up in an attitude of endless possibility, risk and uncertainty very different from the bean-counting control imposed 20 years earlier by Cultural Management 1.0. Whether that experimental, opportunistic approach to risk-taking and decision-making is sustainable will be considered later in this chapter.

Entrepreneurial multitasking

One way of theorising the distinction between artists and cultural entrepreneurs is that whereas artists are concerned primarily with cultural production, cultural entrepreneurs are more likely to extend their activities along the value chain into cultural distribution as well (Rae 2005). According to this argument, the cultural entrepreneur rejects the idea that art is an inherently self-fulfilling and self-sufficient sphere. Cultural entrepreneurs are not satisfied with generating content, they also want to get involved in the process of marketing and exploiting the content they create.

The idea of the cultural entrepreneur challenges the romantic idea of art as an autonomous form of self-expression. It also challenges the classic notion of a value chain in management theory. Porter's value chain forms the basis for his theory of competitive advantage (Porter 1985). One of the first questions any management student will ask about a commercial enterprise will be where the business sits in the value chain. This leads to an analysis of competitive threats from upstream and downstream, as well as from immediate rivals. Cultural entrepreneurs do not 'sit' in the value chain, they range along it. The processes of production and distribution are likely to overlap and interact with each other. By extending along the value chain, cultural entrepreneurship bridges the supposed opposition between 'creatives' and 'suits'; cultural entrepreneurs are responsible for both ends of the process, from the generation of creative content to the management and exploitation of outcomes.

What this means in practice is that the cultural production sector has had to develop an entrepreneurial style of 'self-management' in which managerial and operational tasks overlap. This multitasking culture is driven partly by necessity and partly by a reluctance to delegate creative or managerial responsibilities. For a game developer or a film-maker, creative and managerial tasks are inseparable. Compared to traditional organisational structures, creative and media enterprises are characterised by loose demarcation of roles, flat hierarchies and multiple roles and responsibilities.

This multitasking culture can also be seen as highly creative, according to contemporary theories of creativity. Psychological and sociological theories of creativity suggest that the creative process is characterised by multiple intelligences, switches between 'divergent' and 'convergent' thinking styles, transitions between different, sometimes apparently contradictory, frames of reference. Frank Barron described the ability to tolerate tensions and contradictions as 'ego strength', and found this capacity to be especially pronounced among artists (Barron 1958). Multitasking and self-management can thus be seen as a creative choice as well as a structural necessity.

The ability to handle different modes of thinking and to switch between different ways of seeing and points of view allows creative people to solve problems. When it comes to organisational structure, it is not surprising to find that creative organisations share a similar capacity to accommodate apparently contradictory qualities, and allow and encourage individuals to exchange roles and pursue tasks that cut across the functional divisions of a more traditionally structured firm. Indeed, this entrepreneurial capacity to tolerate overlapping tasks and functions might be a more reliable index of creative capacity than the possession of technical or artistic skills. For a design agency or architectural practice, the ability to manage expectations, interpret a brief and handle the flow of work across a multi-talented team is arguably at least as important as the technical or artistic abilities of individual designers. A designer with excellent communication and project management skills is likely to produce a better result than a technically gifted designer lacking those abilities. Not surprisingly, a majority of design and architectural practices are constituted as partnerships or federations of self-managing individuals rather than as traditionally structured hierarchical firms with clearly defined horizontal and vertical divisions of responsibility.

As with many of the characteristics outlined here, the multitasking culture of cultural entrepreneurship is in part a matter of scale. The creative and media industries are characterised by high levels of self-employment and micro-enterprise (businesses with fewer than ten full-time employees). This is especially true of cultural production. As we will consider in the final part of this chapter, it becomes more difficult to sustain the competitive advantages of cultural entrepreneurship as the organisation grows and matures. The point about scale leads us to our third observation on cultural entrepreneurship, the emphasis on individual agency.

Entrepreneurial individualism

As noted above, the *culture* of cultural entrepreneurship emphasises the agency of individuals. This individualism fitted with the neoliberal turn in the early 2000s' cultural policy, especially in the United Kingdom (McGuigan 2005), placing the burden of risk on individual citizens rather than collective institutions. At the same time, individual cultural entrepreneurs found support in shared networks, often through urban or regional patterns of collaboration and mutual support (Naudin 2015).

Extending beyond the individual business, cultural entrepreneurs are embedded in networks of like-minded collaborators which extend both horizontally and vertically (Bilton 2007, 46–7). Rather than a value chain, the creative sector depends upon a value network of horizontal collaboration between content creators and vertical collaboration between suppliers and distributors. Temporary projects emerge from this pattern and project teams are assembled and redistributed within the wider project ecology (Grabher 2002).

As Naudin found in her study of cultural entrepreneurs in Birmingham (Naudin 2015), these localised networks are an important corrective to the apparent isolation and vulnerability of the solo cultural entrepreneur; indeed, Grabher argues that the basic unit of analysis in the creative industries is not the individual firm, but an ecosystem within which temporary project-based teams coalesce for specific projects then melt back into the broader network (Grabher 2004).

This places some stress upon the multitasking cultural entrepreneur, needing to bridge between multiple roles facing different stakeholders, as well as slipping between the worlds of creativity and commerce (Morris et al. 1993). The cultural entrepreneur has to construct a coherent identity out of this apparent conflict and complexity, not only at the personal level but also at a commercial level. In order to pitch for work and compete in the market, the branded self becomes an important asset to be worked on by 'bohemian entrepreneurs of the self' (Eikhof and Haunschild 2006). Just as businesses construct foundational stories as a basis for their internal culture and external brand, individual cultural entrepreneurs construct heroic, mythical narratives of the self (Gabriel 2004). Erich Poettschacher (2005) has described the importance of 'creation myths' in sustaining the motivation and self-belief of cultural entrepreneurs; often these stories are objectively untrue, but subjectively necessary to shore up the entrepreneur's sense of their own distinctiveness, identity and purpose (Mcgrath, Macmillan and Scheinberg 1992). As with Amabile's studies of motivation in the creative process referenced in Chapter 2, this creative, entrepreneurial identity might be rooted in formative childhood experiences, a view supported by Freudian psychology (Freud 1985) and by Albert Bandura's concept of 'self-efficacy' beliefs (Bandura 1997).

Of course, these identity myths can also have negative consequences. Strong intrinsic motivation and a belief in the unique character of the enterprise are rooted in the experiences of the individual entrepreneur who started the business (Schein 1983). This makes it hard for others to reflect critically on the identity and character of the business, and harder still to change them. Entrepreneurs and enterprises can become so locked into their foundation myths and their self-efficacy beliefs that they are unable to take on board new ideas and new people, to delegate tasks or to confront the need for strategic change. As with Freud's view of individual artistic creativity, the entrepreneurial identity may be essentially dysfunctional, retreating into a mythical past instead of adjusting to the present reality of the business. According to Poettschacher's study of creative businesses in Vienna, the cultural entrepreneur continues to cling to a self-image of heroic exceptionalism even when this belief is no longer objectively justified (Poettschacher 2005). Indeed, the entire concept of 'entrepreneurship' has been criticised as an 'empty signifier', which ignores the extent to which entrepreneurs are more likely to fail than succeed, and which excludes many 'exceptional' individuals who do not fit our heroic narrative of entrepreneurship (Jones and Spicer 2009). The challenge for cultural entrepreneurs adjusting to change and growth will be considered in the next section.

What emerges from this overview of cultural entrepreneurship is the importance of individual identities, stories and agency in shaping Cultural Management 2.0. To return to the beginning, Cultural Management 2.0's core characteristic is the integration of creative and managerial processes and identities. This integration is embodied in the heroic figure of the multitasking, agile, individualistic and autonomous cultural entrepreneur. Yet as has already been suggested in the previous discussion, this self-identity is somewhat fragile, depending on external networks for support and an internal capacity for self-mythologising and self-belief. That integration begins to unravel when the individual cultural entrepreneur transitions to larger and more complex organisational forms.

The problem of growth

Theories of organisational change describe the stages in the evolution of a firm from emergence through growth to maturity and eventual decline (Churchill and Lewis 1983; Greiner 1972). Within these frameworks, entrepreneurship describes the early stages of initiation and emergence. As the firm grows, some of the strengths of the entrepreneur become weaknesses. In particular, the reliance on multitasking individuals becomes increasingly problematic as tasks and roles become more complex, requiring more specialisation and delegation (both internally and externally through outsourcing). The fluid, informal relationships that allowed for rapid decision-making are replaced by more hierarchical, accountable systems and structures. In this context, the maverick entrepreneur, with a shoot-first-ask-questions-later attitude, becomes something of a liability.

The need for a more structured, systematic approach to management takes us back to the debate about strategic planning. Entrepreneurs, including cultural entrepreneurs, are able to make quick intuitive decisions and adapt to uncertain conditions more rapidly than larger, formally structured organisations. This allows them to react quickly to new opportunities and see past existing paradigms to identify new products and markets.

This opportunistic, adaptive approach to decision-making also has some weaknesses. In their discussion of entrepreneurial marketing, Carson et al. (1995) describe the entrepreneur as a 'prisoner to the market' – meaning that entrepreneurs are continually reacting to opportunities in the marketplace rather than taking a step back in order to take a radical leap forward. Entrepreneurs swim with the current, they are captivated by the trends and opportunities stirring around them. This is the flip side of Christenson's argument in *The Innovator's Dilemma*, in which the incumbent businesses are caught in the 'customer trap', locked into their existing customer needs and expectations, preventing them from responding to new opportunities and new technologies (Christensen 1997). Smaller, more agile, entrepreneurial organisations can take advantage of these emerging changes, but they too are trapped by their need to jump onto the next available opportunity before anybody else does. A more deliberate, strategic approach to decision-making is more likely to yield a radical, transformative change – the kind of 'blue ocean' thinking advocated by Kim and Mauborgne (2005). This was Michael Porter's rejoinder to Mintzberg's model of emergent strategy – in a time of uncertainty, for example, when the business environment is being transformed by digital technology, a more analytical deliberate approach is going to yield a more robust future-oriented competitive advantage than chasing the latest fads and fashions (Porter 2001).

How then do organisations, in particular cultural organisations, manage change and growth? As with most of the paradoxes of cultural management, the answer might be found in a bridging between extremes. Entrepreneurial *and* strategic approaches to organisational change should be complementary – the incremental, adaptive changes enacted by agile, entrepreneurial organisations could be steps towards the more transformative, 'big picture' changes enabled through deliberate analysis and strategic planning. There are resonances here with theories of creativity, where incremental changes can be the building blocks towards radical change rather than assuming one is better or worse than another. Margaret Boden draws a distinction between 'exploratory' and 'transformative' creativity (Boden 2004, 75–9). Exploratory creativity takes place within a bounded conceptual space, whereas transformative creativity changes the rules that govern that conceptual space, thereby creating a new paradigm. Other actors – critics, historians, sociologists – might be the ones who define that conceptual space. But for the system to achieve transformation of the conceptual space, all of these elements are needed – 'transformation' does not happen from the outside but from the inside, and exploration is a necessary step towards transformation. Robert Weisberg makes a similar point when analysing the origins of well-known artistic innovations, from Mozart to Picasso – the radical change grows out of a deliberate, incremental process (Weisberg 1993). Applying these insights to entrepreneurship and strategy, the entrepreneur's incremental, opportunistic actions might facilitate a more transformative strategic change.

Theories of organisational change highlight the limitations of different organisational forms in different stages of the organisation's development – there is no perfect model. Successfully negotiating one crisis will lead on to another crisis further down the line, and the organisation must continually evolve to align structure with purpose. Rather than choosing between entrepreneurial and strategic approaches to decision-making and creativity, we should seek out hybrids that bridge between them – entrepreneurial strategists and strategic entrepreneurs. For smaller organisations, this might mean taking a step away from the daily frenzy of action and reaction, making time for a more strategic, longer term conversation. For larger organisations, allowing space for entrepreneurial risk-taking, deviation and experimentation might allow the top-down deliberate strategy to be refreshed, challenged and redirected by those on the operational frontline.

Cultural Management 2.0 – just do it

Of the three theories of cultural management advanced in this book, Cultural Management 2.0 is perhaps the dominant paradigm. Different from Cultural Management 1.0, there is no opposition or residual tension between the 'creative' artist and the managerial 'suit'. Creating the work and delivering and managing the creative outcome are two sides of the same coin. Marketing and management are not separate activities, keeping a respectful distance from the mysteries of creativity, they are integral to the creative process. Indeed, it is only through the delivery and realisation of the creative idea in the mind's eye of the consumer that the creative idea comes to life.

Waiting outside the tent, hoping that artistic creativity will weave its magic, and then picking up the pieces afterwards, is a recipe for stagnation. Artistic creativity, cut off from any concept of strategy, audience or purpose, will become moribund. Managers removed from any contact with the creative process or person will become obstructive bureaucrats. The alternative proposed by Cultural Management 2.0 rests on the integration of artistic invention and managerial intervention. This integration reflects the 'bisociative' theories of the creative process, combining divergent and convergent thinking, intuition and rationality, inspiration and perspiration, creative thinking skills and domain-specific expertise.

The second characteristic of Cultural Management 2.0 is an emphasis on action and execution. We learn by doing, not by planning – Cultural Management 2.0 is accordingly a theory of action. As noted in the final part of this chapter, this faith in heroic entrepreneurial action is a potential blind spot. Sometimes, a more reflective, more analytical approach is called for. Sometimes, the multitasking individual cannot keep up with multiple demands. Cultural Management 2.0 trusts in individuals to make sense of the future but that can result in a pragmatic muddling through, instead of a more transformative, ambitious strategic approach. The other, ethical blind spot is a failure to account for structural inequalities and power imbalances which place the promise of fulfilling, autonomous, resilient, agile creative work beyond the reach of many if not most cultural entrepreneurs.

Cultural Management 2.0 was born out of a moment of change at the turn of the millennium. Responding to fragmentation and technological disruption of the creative and media industries, Cultural Management 2.0 proposed a merging of creative and managerial capabilities, a more holistic integration of cultural production and distribution, and a faith in entrepreneurial individuals who would 'move fast and break things'. That approach was successful up to a point. And the approach was surely a necessary evolutionary step forward from Cultural Management 1.0. But there were casualties and failures. Artists and content creators who could not adapt were left behind. Structural barriers remained high for those with less cultural capital. Many of the businesses and business models which emerged were not sustainable.

The businesses that have survived and grown are the ones that have transitioned to a more strategic approach, tempering entrepreneurial opportunism with longer term vision and leadership. Moreover, a more deliberate, strategic approach to cultural management has the potential to address 'culture' as a shared public good rather than addressing creativity as an individual goal. This applies not just to the growth of creative organisations but to the sector as a whole. The recent pandemic destroyed the careers of many freelance creatives and small creative businesses. Now, more than ever, we need a wider angle view of the cultural sector that can rebuild the infrastructure and linkages on which the entire edifice is constructed.

As the business environment for cultural organisations becomes more complex and unpredictable, Cultural Management 2.0's confident ability to get on with the job may not be enough. The challenges facing leaders of today's cultural organisation are many: the impact of digital technology on business models and value chains; a turbulent postmodern culture where value judgements, consumer identities and aesthetic traditions have become relativised, unstable and contingent. In the cultural and creative industries, such challenges revolve especially around the nature and role of audiences in our digital, postmodern times. They are the new heroes of our creative economy, not the heroic cultural entrepreneur or the genius artist. Tackling the new era of active, co-creative audiences will require a further twist in cultural management – the subject of Chapter 4, Cultural Management 3.0.

References

Bandura, A. (1997). *Self-efficacy: the exercise of control.* New York: W.H. Freeman.

Barrett, F.J. (1988). Creativity and improvisation in jazz and organizations: Implications for organizational learning. *Organization Science*, 9(5), pp. 605–22.

Barron, F. (1958). The psychology of imagination. *Scientific American*, 199(3), pp. 150–69.

Beck, U. (1992). *Risk Society: Towards a New Modernity*. London: Sage.

Bilton, C. (2007): *Management and Creativity: from creative industries to creative management.* (Oxford: Blackwell).

Boden, M.A. (2004). *The Creative Mind: Myths and Mechanisms* (2nd edition). London: Routledge.

Carson, D., Cromie, S., McGowan, P. and Hill, J. (1995). *Marketing and Entrepreneurship in SMEs: An Innovative Approach*. London: Prentice Hall.

Christensen, C. (1997). *The Innovator's Dilemma: When New Technologies Cause Great Firms to Fail*. Boston, MA: Harvard Business School.

Churchill, N. and Lewis, V. (1983). The five stages of small business growth. *Harvard Business Review*, *61*(3), pp. 30–50.

DeFillippi, R.J. and Arthur, M.B. (1998). Paradox in project-based enterprise: The case of film making. *California Management Review*, *40*(2), pp. 125–39.

Eikhof, D.R. and Haunschild, A. (2006). Lifestyle meets market: Bohemian entrepreneurs in creative industries. *Creativity and Innovation Management*, *15*(3), pp. 234–41.

Ellmeier, A. (2003). Cultural entrepreneurialism: On the changing relationship between the arts, culture and employment. *International Journal of Cultural Policy*, 9(1), pp. 3–16.

Freud, S. (1985). Creative writers and daydreaming. In: S. Freud, *Art and Literature: Jensen's Gradiva, Leonardo da Vinci and other works*. Harmondsworth: Penguin, pp. 131–141.

Gabriel, Y. (2004). Stories in organizational research. In: Cassell, C. and Symon, G. (eds.), *Essential Guide to Qualitative Methods in Organizational Research*. London: Sage, pp. 114–26.

Grabher, G. (2002). The project ecology of advertising: Tasks, talents and teams. *Regional Studies*, *36*, pp. 245–62.

Grabher, G. (2004). Learning in projects, remembering in networks? Communality, sociality and connectivity in project ecologies. *European Urban and Regional Studies*, *11*(2), pp. 99–119.

Greiner, L.E. (1972). Evolution and revolution as organizations grow. *Harvard Business Review* 50(4) July/August, pp. 37–46.

Hagoort, G. (2003). *Arts Management: Entrepreneurial Style*. Delft: Eburon.

Hatch, M.J. (1998). The Vancouver Academy of Management Jazz Symposium, jazz as a metaphor for organizing in the 21st century. *Organization Science*, *9*(5), pp. 556–7.

Hatch, M.J. (1999). Exploring the empty spaces of organizing: How improvisational jazz helps redescribe organizational structure. *Organizational Studies*, *20*(1), pp. 75–100.

Hesmondhalgh, D. and Meier, L.M. (2018). What the digitalisation of music tells us about capitalism, culture and the power of the information technology sector. *Information, Communication & Society*, *21*(11), 1555–70.

Jones, C. and Spicer, A. (2009). *Unmasking the Entrepreneur*. Cheltenham: Edward Elgar.

Kim, W.C. and Mauborgne, R. (2005). *Blue ocean strategy: How to create uncontested market space and make the competition irrelevant*. Boston, MA: Harvard Business School Press.

Lampel, J., Lant, T. and Shamsie, J. (2000). Balancing act: Learning from organizing practices in cultural industries. *Organization Science*, *11*(3), pp. 263–9.

McGrath, R.G., MacMillan, I.C. and Scheinberg, S. (1992). Elitists, risk-takers, and rugged individualists? An exploratory analysis of cultural differences between entrepreneurs and non-entrepreneurs. *Journal of Business Venturing*, *7*(2), pp. 115–35.

McGregor, D. (1960). *The Human Side of Enterprise*. New York: McGraw-Hill.

McGuigan, J. (2005). Neo-liberalism, culture and policy. *International Journal of Cultural Policy*, *11*(3), pp. 229–41.

McRobbie, A. (2002). From Holloway to Hollywood: Happiness at work in the new cultural economy. In: du Gay, P. and Pryke, M. (eds.), *Cultural Economy*. London: Sage, pp. 87–114.

McRobbie, A. (2015). *Be Creative: Making a Living in the New Culture Industries*. Cambridge: Polity Press.

Mintzberg, H. (1994). *The Rise and Fall of Strategic Planning*. New York: Prentice Hall.

Mintzberg, H. (1998). Covert leadership: Notes on managing professionals. *Harvard Business Review*, *76*, pp. 140–8.

Mintzberg, H. and McHugh, A. (1985). Strategy formation in an adhocracy. *Administrative Science Quarterly*, *30*, pp. 160–97.

Mintzberg, H. and Waters, J. (1985). Of strategies, deliberate and emergent. *Strategic Management Journal*, *6*, pp. 257–62.

Morris, M.H., Avila, R.A. and Allen, J. (1993). Individualism and the modern corporation: Implications for innovation and entrepreneurship. *Journal of Management*, *19*(3), pp. 595–612.

NACCCE. (1999, May). *All our futures: Creativity, culture and education* (Report to the Secretary of State for Education and Employment and the Secretary of State for Culture, Media and Sport). Retrieved from http://sir kenrobinson.com/pdf/allourfutures.pdf.

Naudin, A. (2015). *Cultural Entrepreneurship: identity and personal agency in the cultural worker's experience of entrepreneurship*. PhD Thesis, University of Warwick.

Naudin, A. (2017). *Cultural Entrepreneurship: the cultural worker's experience of cultural entrepreneurship*. New York: Routledge.

Neelands, J. and Choe, B. (2010). The English model of creativity: Cultural politics of an idea. *International Journal of Cultural Policy*, *16*(3), pp. 287–304.

Negus, K. (1995). Where the mystical meets the market: Creativity and commerce in the production of popular music. *The Sociological Review*, *43*(2), pp. 316–41.

Oakley, K. (2014). Good work? Rethinking cultural entrepreneurship. In: Bilton, C. and Cummings, S. (eds.), *Handbook of Management and Creativity*. Cheltenham: Edward Elgar Publishing.

Parrish, D. (2005). *T-shirts and Suits: A Guide to the Business of Creativity*. Liverpool: Merseyside ACME.

Poettschacher, E. (2005). Strategic creativity: How values, beliefs and assumptions drive entrepreneurs in the creative industries. *International Journal of Entrepreneurship and Innovation*, 6(3), p. 177.

Porter, M. (1985). *Competitive Advantage: Creating and Sustaining Superior Performance*. New York/London: Free Press.

Porter, M. (2001). Strategy and the internet. *Harvard Business Review*, 79(3), pp. 62–78.

Prichard, C. (2002). Creative selves? Critically reading 'creativity' in management discourse. *Creativity and Innovation Management*, 11(4), pp. 265–76.

Rae, D. (2005). Cultural diffusion: A formative process in creative entrepreneurship?. *International Journal of Entrepreneurship and Innovation*, 6(3), pp. 185–7).

Sarasvathy, S. (2001). Causation and effectuation: Towards a theoretical shift from economic inevitability to entrepreneurial contingency. *Academy of Management Review*, 26(2), 243–63.

Schein, E. (1983). The role of the founder in creating organisational culture, *Organisational Dynamics* 12, pp. 13–28.

Schlesinger, P. (2007). Creativity: From discourse to doctrine?. *Screen*, 48(3), pp. 377–387.

Schumpeter, J.A. (1939). *Business Cycles: A Theoretical, Historical and Statistical Analysis of the Capitalist Process*. New York: McGraw Hill.

Stevenson, H.H. (1983[1989]). A perspective on entrepreneurship. In: John J. Kao (ed.), *Entrepreneurship, Creativity & Organization: Text, Cases and Readings*. Englewood Cliffs, NJ: Prentice Hall, pp. 166–77.

Tusa, J. (2003). *On Creativity: Interviews Exploring the Creative Process*. London: Methuen.

Wallin, J. (2006). *Business Orchestration: Strategic Leadership in the Era of Digital Convergence*. Chichester: John Wiley.

Weick, K.E. (1998). Improvisation as a mindset for organizational analysis. *Organization Science*, 9(5), pp. 543–55.

Weisberg, R.W. (1993). *Creativity: Beyond the Myth of Genius*. New York: W. H. Freeman.

Wright, D. (2018). "Hopeful work" and the creative economy. In: Martin, L. and Wilson, N. (eds.), *The Palgrave Handbook of Creativity at Work*. Cham: Palgrave Macmillan, pp. 311–25.

4 Cultural Management 3.0

Managing co-creation through vulnerable leadership

Unpredictability is a defining feature of the media, cultural and creative industries. Other sectors might face similarly unpredictable production processes and market environments – many working in technology could claim to share comparable dilemmas. But uncertainty is wired into the definition of the creative industries through the production of meaning. Because creative industries are producing symbolic goods, where ideas, information and emotion must be experienced and interpreted in order to be realised, it is up to consumers to complete the circuit of meaning.

Over the last 15 years, consumers have played an increasingly active role in co-creating this meaning. Part of this can be attributed to new technologies of communication. Online social media not only allow information to be instantly shared, copied and reshared on a massive scale, they also enable consumers to comment, tweak and reframe content in their own image. Information flows both ways. This is the essence of 'web 2.0' – it is also the challenge for Cultural Management 3.0.

Of course, active or 'creative' consumption is not new – in 1934, the American philosopher John Dewey argued that when we look at a painting, we go through a creative process to make sense of what it means. Dewey described this as an 'aesthetic experience' and suggested that the viewer is going through a similar experience to the artist who made the painting (Dewey 1958). But today's fans are no longer just looking at the picture, they are sharing selfies and putting themselves in the frame.

Similarly, media scholars have long argued that audiences are active, not passive, absorbers of meaning (Liebes and Katz 1990; Katz and Lazarsfeld 1955). But today's experience economy takes that active role further. In *The Experience Economy*, Pine and Gilmore (1999) argue that the product is no longer centre stage, it functions more like the props and scenery, which allow audiences to perform their own drama. Taking this further, the business models of the big tech companies are

DOI: 10.4324/9781003009184-4

no longer investing in content, instead seeking to commodify consumption. All of this serves to devalue content and content creators, whilst foregrounding the process of consumption.

Theories of media flow which highlighted the autonomy of media consumers have been absorbed into theories of fandom and we-media. Using digital tools and online social networks to co-create content, fans have blurred the line between producer and consumer. 'Produsers' and 'prosumers' play an important part in the value chain of the creative economy – they don't just complete the circuit of meaning they often initiate it.

Cultural Managements 1.0 and 2.0 were attempts to manage the relationship between creativity and commerce. In version 1.0, these were regarded as opposite and separate. Cultural Management 1.0 combined bureaucratic control over the business of creativity, with laissez-faire detachment from the creative process itself. This separation was reflected in Amabile's approach to managing creativity, through clear strategic goals and 'autonomy around the process'. Cultural Management 2.0 instead assumed that there was no contradiction between creativity and business, between culture and management. This integration was embodied in the cultural entrepreneur, slipping comfortably between creative and managerial roles.

Both of these earlier models of cultural management assumed that cultural production and dissemination comprise a self-contained process. The work of the artist, manager or cultural entrepreneur is complete once the creative product or service has been launched into the world. But now, managing the processes of co-creation extends cultural management further. Now, it is necessary to understand and engage with the audiences and fans who are playing with that cultural content, recreating it, ripping it and remixing it.

As noted in Chapter 3, this new model of cultural management was integral to the big tech companies (Google, Amazon, Meta, Apple; Baidu, Alibaba, Tencent), which have built their business models around the commodification of consumption and consumers. The traditional intermediaries that they have displaced – record labels, publishers, broadcasters, newspapers, film studios – were much slower to adapt. Record labels initially responded to Napster by aggressively defending their intellectual property (IP) rights – first by suing the online file-sharing networks, then by threatening to sue their own consumers. The fact that most consumers and many musicians resented the copyright owned by record labels made this strategy doubly unpopular. It took Apple, a tech company, to launch the first successful music download service; instead of working together to counter the threat, the major labels competed to set up their own separate proprietary services (Sony-BMG went from suing Napster, via the Recording Industry Association of America, to attempting to partner with them).

It's no surprise that traditional cultural organisations found it difficult to adapt to the new media landscape. Not only was their entire business model invested in controlling and managing the flow of content, they also – unlike the new digital intermediaries – retained a romantic faith in the intrinsic value of creative content, believed in the integrity of IP, and trusted in their own abilities as effective and necessary components in the value chain: nurturing and developing new talent, filtering and directing the best content, and matching products with markets.

Cultural Management 3.0 recognises that, whilst much of this work of Cultural Managements 1.0 and 2.0 remains valuable and necessary, it is not enough. We need to find ways of managing and integrating the consumption of creative content with production. We need to consider consumers or 'fans' as participants, not recipients. We need to recognise that the best ideas might come not from product innovation or entrepreneurial adaptation, but from the uses and users outside our organisation. That requires a more humble and vulnerable approach to management and leadership.

Open innovation

'Open innovation' grew out of 'open source' innovation in the technology sector, whereby companies like Linux released beta versions of software and invited users to adapt the code to suit their needs, then fed these user-generated modifications back into the software. In the cultural and creative industries, games developers have used a similar tactic by integrating player modifications ('mods') back into gameplay. And beyond technology or creative sectors, companies like Lego have facilitated consumer creativity, incentivising users to contribute to the design of models and kits and learning from user-generated content on YouTube to design games and other spin-off products. As Chesbrough and others have indicated, open innovation is a cooperation based on mutual benefit – both the users and the business benefit in multiple ways, not only through product development but also through the marketing and dissemination of innovations. User-led innovation generates marketing 'buzz' for the core business (and vice versa), opens out new business models and reaches out to new markets or user communities (Chesbrough et al. 2006).

One of the barriers to open innovation in the cultural and creative industries has been copyright infringement. Copyright is the means by which content creators can earn money from their creations, and also allows copyright owners to cross-subsidise product development from successful products in the market. Allowing users to hack that product and reinvent it threatens not only the copyright holder's economic rights (revenue streams) but also their moral rights (the author's right to be identified as the creator of the work). With business models increasingly tilting away from products to branded experiences and customer relationships, the direct revenues from copyrighted products may have become less important. But when 'content' is increasingly being given away for free (or being taken for free by illegal means), it is more important than ever for the copyright holder to profit from the brands and relationships constructed around that content. Consequently, the moral rights of copyright – the right of the author to be identified as such – have arguably become more important than economic rights. Digital rights management offers a way of inscribing ownership not only into the original content, but also into derivative products. With the increasing use of creative commons licences, this is likely to become an increasingly important factor in copyright enforcement.

Against this background, digital fandom has opened up new frontiers in consumer creativity. E L James' *Fifty Shades of Grey* began life as a work of fan fiction based on Stephanie Meyers' *Twilight* books – with over 15 million sales, the new franchise has sold nearly as many copies as the 'original' series, as well as launching a series of successful film adaptations. In gaming, a number of fan 'mods' have added a second life to games, from The Dark Mod and Doom RL (based on Doom) to Black Mesa (based on Half Life) to a host of fan mash-ups of 'retro' Pokemon, Street Fighter and Super Mario titles. Game developers like Valve and Capcom have embraced fan games, investing in and hiring fan developer teams like Crowbar, Totem Arts and PlayerUnknown, commercially releasing the games and using fan versions to reanimate their own franchises.

As Matt Hills (2002) observes, fandom can take us beyond this linear model of adapting one product into another, towards a more expansive model where multiple versions coexist. Instead of a hierarchy between the 'original' and 'fan' versions, there is a fan multiverse where layers of meaning accumulate. The BBC TV series *Sherlock* illustrates this interplay between 'original' and 'adaptation' with the later episodes responding playfully to fan fiction and fan theories – to the point where these later episodes have been criticised as 'fan service', sacrificing the integrity of the show to the accumulated alternative readings by fans and casting the 'auteur' as just another fan. This leads to a debate about the legitimacy of fan products – do we still need to distinguish between 'real' fiction and 'fan fiction', especially for a show like *Sherlock*, which is itself a less than faithful adaptation of another fiction (Conan Doyle's *Adventures of Sherlock Holmes*)?

Fan fiction and open innovation represent an expansive version of user-generated content which potentially threatens the status of content creators (Hesmondhalgh 2010), especially given the already precarious nature of much creative work. However, it is worth emphasising that the threat comes not so much from fans themselves as from the platforms which drive consumers towards 'free' user-generated content at the expense (literally) of 'legitimate' sources. Corporations like Google/YouTube and Meta/Facebook consistently lobby against copyright protection and seem slow to take down material that infringes authors' rights. As Hills argues, the partnership between fans and artists can be more productive and more equal – to the point where the distinction between them can seem artificial.

In relation to cultural management, it is important to recognise open source innovation as a partnership of equals. As von Hippel (2006) has observed, user innovation networks help to 'democratise' innovation, with 'lead users' helping to seed second-generation innovations across a user community or network. Lead users are plugged into more specialised needs and wants of their respective communities and can adapt and redirect innovations to users. This network effect blurs the hierarchy between professional and amateur, expert and neophyte, producer and user. Learning from the 'wisdom of crowds' requires a humility from the 'original' creator, accepting that others may be capable of discovering and realising new forms of value, and that the 'adaptation' might be as valuable as the 'innovation'. Rather than attempting to control these next-generation innovations, von Hippel argues that businesses should be trying to facilitate user-led innovation by providing tools and resources and responding positively to user-led initiatives.

This idea of cooperating with potential competitors challenges a fundamental principle of business management, the pursuit of competitive advantage. It is clear that there are varying degrees of 'openness' in open innovation, within firms as well as between them. Apple, for example, has become more open in its partnerships with music creators and app developers, whilst retaining its more closed 'walled garden' attitude to chip manufacture and hardware. Apple's continued insistence upon proprietary accessories from chargers to USB ports, whilst irritating to consumers, reflects a reluctance to surrender control and revenues in what it views as the most lucrative part of the business. So, Apple's software development partnerships are an open system, but hardware remains 'closed'. But even Apple is learning to compromise from its earlier defence of a 'branded ecosystem' and has opened up to partners and collaborators. This points us towards the first characteristic of Cultural Management 3.0 – learning to follow not lead the creative process.

The learning organisation

Throughout this book, the unpredictable nature of the creative process has been presented as especially challenging for cultural managers. One solution, floated under Cultural Management 1.0 in Chapter 2, was for the manager to simply resign from managing the process and focus on managing the outcomes. In this chapter, we are considering that the process does not end with the 'outcomes' – there is a post-outcome phase of creativity where users reinvent and adapt the product in unexpected directions. In Cultural Management 3.0, this 'post-creative' phase of adaptation and redirection needs to be looped back into the cultural manager's thinking.

Peter Senge has described the learning organisation as a continually evolving system, which embeds innovators and managers in teams and communities where they can continually adapt their thinking (Senge 2006). There are echoes here of systems theories of creativity, where individual creativity is embedded in collective systems (the field and the domain) which shape and direct the outcomes (Csikszentmihalyi 1988). Senge describes a feeling among team members of 'being part of something larger than themselves' (Senge 2006, 13) and needing to learn from *all* parts of the organisation. In Cultural Management 3.0, this holistic mindset extends to audiences and users outside the organisation too. Senge also emphasised the need to take a long-term view of feedback – short-term failure can lead to long-term success. That long-term orientation is at odds with a purely commercial mindset – a financial loss could still be a productive failure, helping the organisation to learn and change. This could be applied to fan cultures – somebody misappropriating and misinterpreting your IP could be considered a loss in the short term (copyright infringement, loss of earnings), but could deliver a longer term gain (relationship with users, building brand awareness, opening new creative pathways and markets).

Senge has been criticised for presenting a utopian, idealistic model that is difficult to implement or even identify in real organisations. Yet his work was prescient in relation to fashionable areas like design thinking. At its simplest, design thinking means beginning the production process from an understanding of consumers' needs and uses – this principle takes Senge's ideas about openness and dialogue (Senge 2006, 10) and applies them to openness and dialogue with the customer. In the context of cultural products and Cultural Management 3.0, that dialogue focuses not just on customer needs but on the audience's interpretation of symbolic meaning. Understanding how users will interpret and reinterpret texts, weaving new meanings of their own, opens up the co-creative possibilities of Cultural Management 3.0.

In *Design-driven Innovation*, Roberto Verganti argues that instead of 'user-centred innovation' we should pursue 'radical innovation of meanings' (Verganti 2009, 21). Consumers value products for what they mean, not what they do – and to this extent *every* product has symbolic meaning. Focusing on meaning over function, on the 'how' rather than the 'what', means 'shining a spotlight on the cultural dimension of the product' (Verganti 2009, 38). It also means ignoring market research (as Lord Reith observed of the BBC audience, 'few know what they want, fewer what they need') and avoiding the 'customer trap' identified by Christensen (1997). Incumbent businesses are more likely to be 'user-led' rather than 'design-driven'. Verganti claims that there are three approaches to innovation – technology push (relying on Research and Development), market pull (user-led) and 'design push' (reimagining future needs) (Verganti 2009, 55–7). These three approaches map onto the models of Cultural Managements 1.0, 2.0 and 3.0, respectively.

Design-driven innovation is harder to imitate than user-centred or producer-driven innovation because it does not just deliver a new piece of technology or a new service – it creates a new 'archetype of meaning' (Verganti 2009, 95). Reaching that goal requires 'basic research on sociocultural models' (Verganti 2009, 109) – not market research. The radical innovation of meanings is proposed by the designer, not the consumer – but by anticipating future uses and interpretations, the designer is learning from customers at a deeper level of analysis.

Cultural Management 3.0 does not attempt to control consumer creativity, but it attempts to anticipate and design a space within which consumer creativity can occur. Learning organisations and design-led innovation provide a framework of possibilities, not a self-contained outcome, and invite users (audiences, users, fans) to play. As Verganti indicates, building this framework is the work of the designer, building alliances with social analysts, cultural critics and futurologists, and imagining future audience interpretations and subjectivities. These connections have the potential to extend the learning organisation's horizons well beyond the possibilities of internal R&D or external customer research.

Senge's 'learning organisation' is invoked here because his vision of a holistic, extensive view of the organisation extending outwards into broader systems and relationships accords with Cultural Management

3.0. 'Learning' reflects Senge's understanding of systems thinking, based on the idea of 'feedback' which connects up and makes sense of different inputs and which aims for a long-term view of success and failure (Senge 2006, 74–90). 'Learning' then is partly about 'listening', but also recognising the connections which join up production and consumption, future meanings and present design, short-term failure and long-term success. In relation to Cultural Management 3.0, Senge also describes a systems model of creativity and innovation, where future uses and behaviours by users are integral to the long-term value (and meaning) of a cultural product.

Learning from the tribe

Verganti emphasises that it is the designer/producer, not the consumer, who drives the innovation process. In order to imagine future innovations of meaning, that process is customer-focused. But it is emphatically not customer-led.

Theories of postmodern marketing suggest a different relationship between producers and consumers. Drawing on postmodern theory – the instability of meaning, value and identity in contemporary society – postmodern marketing emphasises the need to follow rather than lead the consumer's creation of meaning (Cova 1996; Goulding et al. 2013). Arguing that consumption is shaped not by clearly defined demographic categories and directly articulated needs, postmodern marketing attempts to unravel the 'hidden' aspects of cultural identity and to include the 'invisible' members of the tribe (Cova and Cova 2002). The 'tribe' becomes the focus instead of market segments or 'target markets'. Cova and Cova gives the example of roller-skaters in Paris, and show that the most successful way for marketers to reach this group was to facilitate the skaters' community, connections and relationships, creating spaces for interaction rather than attempting to intervene or sell to them directly (Cova and Cova 2002).

Many of the examples used in discussions of postmodern marketing are 'cultural' or 'subcultural' groupings – heavy metal fans, skateboarders, surfers, vinyl record collectors. The emphasis on the cultural dimension of consumption, especially the ways in which we actively create (or co-create) meanings, the subjectivity of value judgements, the way in which identities are shaped by our immediate experiences of events and gatherings with like-minded others, all resonate strongly with the nature of cultural products. The argument that the marketer should attempt to follow rather than lead this process fits also with the model of Cultural Management 3.0.

Practically speaking, this means a more indirect approach from the marketer. Understanding how groups are structured, where are the key influencers and what draws people together requires a more immersive, ethnographic approach than traditional market research. The product's value is not intrinsic nor is it fixed to any standards of quality, rather it must be understood in relation to its meaning for this community, at this time, and the specific relationships it enables within the tribe, referred to by Cova as 'linking value' (Cova 1997). Cultural Management 3.0 likewise means acknowledging the wisdom of the tribe and laying aside the traditional armoury of analysis, measurement, prediction and top-down strategy. This is a far cry from the confident 'design push' of Apple or Alessi. To engage with the tribe, the cultural manager must step down from the podium and mingle with the crowds on the floor.

Surrendering to the wisdom of the tribe is not without risk – customers might 'hijack' the brand and take the product in unexpected and unwelcome directions. We have seen both sides of this in the fashion industry with brands like Burberry, Nike or Fred Perry embraced by various subcultures for better or worse. There is also the risk that the tribal marketer will cultivate an engagement with the tribe but never succeed in converting that engagement into action, like an older relative hanging out with the cool kids (and buying all the drinks). All of this can leave postmodern marketing looking foolish – a clever theory with no clear steps to implementation.

Yet postmodern marketing remains an important ingredient in Cultural Management 3.0, mainly because it reflects a change in attitude and approach. Compared to the confident certainties of Cultural Managements 1.0 and 2.0, there is a new acceptance of the marketer's limitations. The meanings and values of the cultural product are continually being renegotiated. The attitudes and identities of consumers, especially cultural consumers, are in flux, contingent upon who they are with, who they want to be with and who they want to become rather than who they are. Cultural products have always been aspirational – a way of rewriting our identities and entering new worlds. One response to this uncertainty is to give up – to just 'go with the flow'. Postmodern marketing offers an alternative, an attempt to make sense of emergent patterns, look into the swirl of big data for the connection between individual behaviours and build a picture of a changing world. Cultural Management 3.0 shares this spirit of improvisation and sensemaking – not pretending to be able to predict audience behaviours, but not giving up on the relationship either.

Reducing Cultural Management 3.0 to a methodology is difficult – techniques like data scraping, 'cool-hunting', brand communities, building partnerships with KOLs (Key Opinion Leaders), all manifest the learning/listening approach being advocated here. But in order to understand what they do, we might first need to consider who cultural managers 3.0 are, starting with the nature of leadership.

Leading from the back

Trait-based theories of leadership, like person-based theories of creativity, tend to collapse in on themselves once we start listing the many, often contradictory, qualities needed to produce the perfect leader. Yet belief in the power of leadership takes the pressure off everybody else – if one person is responsible for the success of the organisation or project, others will be rewarded or punished only to the extent they follow that leader's directions. This may be why, despite overwhelming evidence that there is no such thing as the perfect leader, many still choose to believe in it (or him – this archetype is usually gendered male). Charismatic leaders succeed in part because their followers attribute success to the leader and failure to themselves. At the same time, charismatic leaders squeeze the initiative out of those they lead, sometimes unintentionally, making it harder for anybody to challenge their leadership, still less succeed them. As discussed in Chapter 3, cultural entrepreneurs often possess the charisma of charismatic leadership without the leadership – the shortcomings of the charismatic, heroic individual become more exposed as the organisation grows in scale and complexity.

Charismatic leadership is only an extreme expression of a more widespread assumption that leaders are 'different' or special – and that their heroic status is framed by the organisational hierarchy. The hierarchical distinction between leaders and managers harks back to Mintzberg's critique of strategic planning discussed in Chapter 3 – by placing strategic planning and the leaders who strategize on a pedestal, we disconnect them from the operational realities. Leaders do strategy, managers do operations. Leaders set the direction, managers ensure directions are followed. In the cultural sector, especially in the performing arts, leaders often do possess high levels of charisma, drawing on their star quality as accomplished performers, artists or directors. As with the entrepreneur turned leader, artist-leaders are not always good at delegating and can have a toxic effect on those around them (Nisbett and Walmsley 2016).

Transformational leadership is an attempt to lead not by directive but by inspiring others to buy into a shared vision. According to 'situational' theories of leadership, there is no perfect model of leadership, the best fit will depend on the situation of the leader, the follower and the organisation. Transformational leadership reflects a more evolved relationship between leaders and followers, where the organisation is more mature and in which followers have developed a higher level of commitment and skill. At this point, transactional leadership – the carrot and the stick to reward or punish compliance and non-compliance – is no longer necessary or effective. By inspiring followers to find their own self-fulfilment in the task, transformational leadership will engage a stronger sense of purpose and encourage followers to take the lead themselves.

Considering the correlation between creativity and intrinsic motivation, as discussed in Chapter 2, there is an obvious fit between transformational leadership and the 'situation' of the cultural and creative industries. High levels of personal motivation and task fulfilment are most likely to bring out the strongest creative performance. Again, we can find examples of this in the cultural sector, where leadership roles are often distributed across different people and the success of the organisation is driven by collective leadership, not an individual leader.

The opposite of charismatic leadership might be vulnerable leadership. Whereas the ego of the charismatic leader overwhelms the leadership potential of others, the vulnerable leader's lack of ego creates a space in which other ideas of leadership can take shape. Simply by acknowledging their own uncertainty and vulnerability, vulnerable leaders invite others to step forward and take responsibility. This acceptance of inadequacy is an important ingredient in Senge's learning organisation. One of the principles of the learning organisation is a willingness to learn, and what Senge describes as 'personal mastery' requires 'an awareness of ignorance and incompetence' (Senge 2006, 133). The best-known advocate of 'vulnerable' leadership, Brené Brown, frames vulnerability in terms of 'courage' – it is only by confronting fear, failure and uncertainty that we can develop authentic courage, connection and meaning (Brown 2018). The vulnerable leader will develop these qualities by exposing herself emotionally and intellectually to criticism and negativity – and will also cultivate honest communication with those around her. She encourages her readers to discard their 'armour' in order to develop a more open connection with colleagues (and with themselves) (Brown 2018).

Again, considering the high levels of uncertainty and risk in the cultural and creative industries (the statistical inevitability that failures will outnumber successes by multiples of ten or 20 times), vulnerable leadership surely has an important part to play. Learning from failure, accepting uncertainty, giving and receiving negative feedback (without taking or giving offence) are all essential skills for anybody working in the cultural and creative sector.

At the heart of vulnerable leadership is the idea of honest, open communication – what Brené Brown calls 'the rumble'. Much of Brown's *Dare to Lead* book is based on her experience of running workshops with leaders and the book includes exercises designed to strip away defensive mechanisms and engage in honest, authentic communication. This is perhaps the core of Cultural Management 3.0 – the need to listen, not only to our colleagues and to our own inner feelings and uncertainties, but also to our audiences and users.

Listen carefully

Whether we are enabling the learning organisation, tuning in to the wisdom of the tribe, trusting others to complete our innovations, tapping into 'radical innovations of meaning', or identifying the patterns of emergent strategy, 'listening' has emerged as both a metaphor and a practical technique for managing 21st-century organisations. Practising deep, mindful, attentive listening is the way to draw out a deeper level of thinking and insight in ourselves and others. As Nancy Kline argues in *A Time to Think*, 'the quality of your attention determines the quality of other people's thinking' (Kline 1999, 30).

This kind of attention takes more than a peremptory invitation for 'any questions' or formulaic exercises in market research and consultation. As Verganti emphasises, people don't always know what they want and, as in many personal relationships, people don't always say what they mean. Listening attentively means building trust and building relationships. Brown emphasises that what she calls 'vulnerability' is 'relational' – it means acknowledging the challenges we face in addressing each other honestly, as a first step towards building a more truthful connection. This is the opposite of weakness. For some years, these skills have been undervalued in MBA curricula, partly because the kind of experiential learning advocated by Brown is difficult to replicate in a lecture hall, but perhaps too because of a gendered assumption that these are 'soft skills', a term Brown firmly rejects (Brown 2018, 15).

Attention requires a certain humility and self-awareness, a realisation that the leader is also a follower. In relation to Cultural Management 3.0, listening opens up the creative process to the iterative loops of user co-creation, and draws them back into the circuit of meaning and value that allows creativity to gather momentum.

We have conceded much of the so-called attention economy to big tech companies which harvest consumer data and exploit consumer relationships to sell advertising. This has led to a justifiable perception that these powerful intermediaries are the monopoly capitalists of attention – by allowing this monopoly to grow unchecked, we have made the platform owners more powerful and more valuable than the content they use to draw us in (Zuboff 2019; Srnicek 2017). But attention is not only a resource to be mined for profit, it can also be generative, providing space for new ideas and perspectives. Innovation is more likely to flourish in a *culture* of attention than in an attention *economy*.

For all the sophistication of algorithmic culture, these technologies are incapable of the kind of emotional intelligence and intimacy that allows for real connection and relationships between audiences and artists. For vulnerable leadership, for co-creation, for authentic connection, small is beautiful. Of course, these relationships can be recreated algorithmically, and fans can be engaged in pseudo-personalised connections with stars. But if given the choice, most fans will prefer to interact with an artist than with an algorithm (Løvlie and Waern 2022). The enthusiastic return to live performance after the Covid-19 pandemic highlighted the importance of that personalised, direct connection at the heart of the creative economy. By attending to audiences as creative equals, Cultural Management 3.0 can reposition attention as a source of innovation not just a source of revenue.

Recentring Cultural Management 3.0

Thus far, Cultural Management 3.0 has been described as an expansive movement – widening the circle to include users and audiences, delegating control from the core to the periphery. Vulnerable leadership opens itself to challenges and questions from below, authors and content creators allow others to reimagine and redirect their work. All of this has been described as a concession of control, from centre to margins.

However, it is important that this concession is not interpreted as an abdication of responsibility. Vulnerability is not weakness, it is a way of building trust, encouraging more authentic communication and engaging others in resolving problems. As well as opening out, Cultural Management 3.0 is a regathering movement, drawing different strands together. Karl Weick has described the role of leadership as a social process of sensemaking, bringing different perceptions and experiences together into a shared narrative (Weick 1995; Maitlis and Sonenshein 2010; Søderberg 2003). At the same time, as encouraging new perspectives and perceptions, sensemaking builds frameworks for shared understanding.

A current example of this might be post-Covid-19 recovery in the arts. One effect of the pandemic was to break up established supply chains and relationships, exposing structural weaknesses and inequalities in the arts ecosystem. Freelance artists and small business were especially badly affected, with many forced to leave the profession they loved in order to seek financially secure work elsewhere. During the early stages of the pandemic, there was a sense of new possibilities and alternatives ('building back better'). During the later stages of the pandemic and the 'post-pandemic' period (albeit we are not yet definitively 'post' Covid-19), there was an impetus to return to how things had been before, to get 'back to normal'. The challenge for the cultural sector has been to take stock of what has been learned, to identify the vulnerabilities and the opportunities in order to rethink and redirect. Opening out and vulnerability was the first stage. The second stage of rebuilding has not yet happened, not least because any reconstruction or sensemaking will require resources, vision and common purpose – none of which has yet come forward. Letting a thousand flowers bloom, allowing others the freedom to co-create, will only work if a culture is created which provides recognition and resources to the co-creators, and draws those on the fringes back into the centre. In the context of UK cultural policy, all of that is expensive and requires leadership. These resources are in short supply in a sector which has been undermined politically and economically over many years, and which is facing further headwinds from austerity, economic crisis and politicised attacks (the so-called 'culture wars' and 'war on woke').

A historical example of this centre-periphery pattern might be the community arts movement of the late 1970s and 1980s. Here was an opening out of the closed system of cultural production to include previously marginalised voices and a 'democratisation' of cultural institutions. Yet the aim of the community arts movement was not just to gain recognition and resources for peripheral communities and cultures, it was also to transform the centre. According to campaigners like Owen Kelly, this 'storming of the citadel' never happened – instead the community arts movement was decentralised, passed over to regional funding bodies and marginalised as 'alternative' or 'minority' art forms, leaving the UK cultural establishment more or less intact, with its London postcodes, and its confident, privileged position at the head of the 'great tradition', relatively untroubled (Kelly 1984). At a micro-level too, according to my own experience of community arts in the 1980s, participants did not just want the community artist to endorse their efforts, they wanted access to the insights and skills of the 'professional' artist. They wanted to be part of the cultural conversation with 'serious' artists and organisations, not to be patronised on the periphery. They wanted product – a picture in the gallery, a show on the stage – not endless 'process'. Don't just shine a light on those outside the circle, bring them into the centre!

From the perspective of creativity theory, co-creation needs not only to be an expansive, opening movement, but also redirected inwards to transform the concepts and values of the 'bounded conceptual space' at the centre. This is the 'transformative' creativity described by Margaret Boden, which is referenced in Chapter 3 (Boden 2004, 75–9). We collaborate with others not just to explore alternative realities but to challenge our own values and beliefs. Opening out to innovative ideas and new voices is the first step – using these to transform the dominant paradigm completes the circuit.

As discussed in Chapter 1, cultural management is a paradoxical or 'bisociative' process. The paradox at the core of Cultural Management 3.0 is that the expansive opening to engage collaborative creativity is nevertheless supported by structures and resources to enable those external partnerships to be drawn inwards and reintegrated with the organisational core.

Delegating power from the known to the unknown, from the established to the emergent, is a challenging process because it threatens vested interests. That requires not only a concession of power outwards and downwards, but also constructing frameworks that connect those on the outside with those on the inside. Opening up new pathways for talent, providing spaces for new voices to be heard, building new more democratic governance structures for our cultural institutions, will take time, ingenuity and resources (including financial resources). Delegating power downwards to localised communities and individuals, investing in emerging talent, building connections between audiences, communities and artists, will also require a political shift. And Cultural Management 3.0 will have a cultural dimension, as Weick noted in his sensemaking theory: building the shared understandings which allow core ideas and values to be transformed and weaving different voices into a shared narrative or common culture. Leaders can build this transformative culture by connecting disparate voices and building channels which allow values and strategies at the core of the organisation to be influenced and transformed by experimental activities, individuals and subcultures from outside.

Cultural Management 3.0 and cultural commons

Cultural Management 3.0 is an attempt to engage with wider patterns of co-creation beyond the initial exchange between artist and audience. Fandom, open innovation, tribal marketing and the communities and relationships which accumulate around them have become increasingly integral to our future creative economy. If these behaviours are going to be allowed the space to flourish, challenge and redefine authorial intentions, they cannot be 'managed' directly from the centre. But theories of vulnerability and deep listening suggest that there may be ways of nurturing the relationships which underpin them. As Rifkin observed at the start of this millennium, relationships have replaced transactions as the building blocks of the new economy (Rifkin 2000). In the cultural sector, we see this transition in the growing importance of subscriptions to magazines, theatres and cinemas; the shift from buying and owning MP3s, CDs and DVDs to 'unlimited' streaming services; the increasing time artists are expected to devote to social media, blogging and personal appearances beyond their core creative work. All of these business models and behaviours are built on relationships rather than transactions.

Relationships in this attention economy have until now been monopolised by the new intermediaries – platforms, broadband providers, social media services, aggregators – but they can be reclaimed by cultural organisations. We need to listen – really listen – to our audiences. We also need an approach to management which is more open minded, less directive and more willing to learn, not just from audiences and users, but also from those inside our organisations. As Web 2.0 moved towards a more interactive, collective use of online resources, Cultural Management 3.0 invites us to lead from below, manage upwards and adapt to the unexpected.

Cultural Management 3.0 is better conceptualised as organisational culture than as organisational structure. Values like trust, honesty, authenticity and tolerance will be more resilient than fixed systems and strategies when coping with risk and uncertainty, and better able to accommodate the wisdom of the tribe or crowd. Again, such an approach resonates with cultural organisations where 'management by values' regularly trumps 'management by objectives'.

Recently, UNESCO has suggested that culture should be included as a strategic development goal in its own right – as a 'sector', not just a 'vector' to achieve other goals in education or health. Central to this argument is the idea of culture as a public good – a non-rivalrous set of products and services, the sharing of which increases rather than diminishes its value. This idea can be traced back to Thomas Jefferson and his argument that sharing knowledge increases rather than reduces its worth – like using one candle or 'taper' to light another (Hyde 2006). This challenges the notion that IP is a private possession to be exploited, proposing instead a cultural commons open to all. As already noted, conceding private IP rights in pursuit of a public good might be painful or threatening to those who earn their income from cultural production. Jefferson's proposal was for a balance between public and private interests – a balance that many critics argue has swung too far in favour of corporate rights holders and intermediaries (Lessig 2015). And the ideal of a cultural commons is also complicated by different levels of access to available public goods and rivalries over the production and consumption of 'non-rivalrous' products. Alice Borchi (2018) identifies cultural commons as a site of struggle in which cultural rights and resources are reappropriated or reclaimed. Managing these paradoxes and complexities will require leadership. Persuading some to concede private rights in pursuit of the common good and providing a compelling vision of culture as a shared public good are central to the task of Cultural Management 3.0.

Cultural Management 1.0 imported the assumptions of orthodox management into the cultural sector. The result was an often dysfunctional imposition of old-fashioned corporate business methods on top of artistic processes. Cultural Management 2.0 represented a more harmonious marriage between entrepreneurial creativity and creative entrepreneurship, with a new flexibility enabling a proliferation of creative and media enterprise at the start of the millennium. Cultural Management 3.0 takes us full circle, with the co-creative practices of users, fans and 'the people formerly known as the audience' taking centre stage, and managers now having to listen and learn rather than leading from the centre.

Yet each of these models has been flawed. Chapter 2 described the dysfunctional opposition between managers and creatives at the heart of Cultural Management 1.0. The more integrated alignment between creativity and management under Cultural Management 2.0 worked well for small entrepreneurial enterprises but began to break up as organisations grew and matured. And Cultural Management 3.0 creates a space of possibilities but also a potential for chaos and disintegration with consumers threatening to squeeze out the autonomy and authority of cultural producers (abetted by platforms that have their own reasons for prioritising consumption over production, and by governments that use populist rhetoric to challenge cultural 'elites') (Keen 2011).

All three of these models offer only partial solutions to the challenges confronting cultural management. Rather than setting them against each other, it might be more effective to seek a balance between them. Chapter 5 of this book will attempt to weave them together, considering how different models of management might be applied to different stages in the creative process.

References

Borchi, A. (2018). Culture as commons: Theoretical challenges and empirical evidence from occupied cultural spaces in Italy. *Cultural Trends, 27*(1), pp. 33–45.

Brown, B. (2018). *Dare to Lead: Brave Work, Tough Conversations, Whole Hearts.* London: Penguin/Vermilion.

Chesbrough, H., Vanhaverbeke, W. and West, J. (2006). *Open Innovation: Researching a New Paradigm.* Oxford: Oxford University Press.

Christensen, C. (1997). *The Innovator's Dilemma: When New Technologies Cause Great Firms to Fail.* Boston, MA: Harvard Business School.

Cova, B. (1996). The postmodern explained to managers: Implications for marketing. *Business Horizons, 39*(6), 15–23.

Cova, B. (1997). Community and consumption: Towards a definition of the "linking value" of products or services. *European Journal of Marketing, 31*(3/4), 297–316.

Cova, B. and Cova, V. (2002). Tribal marketing: The tribalisation of society and its impact on the conduct of marketing. *European Journal of Marketing, 35*(5/6), 595–620.

Csikszentmihalyi, M. (1988). Society, Culture and Person: A systems view of creativity. In: R.J. Sternberg (ed.), *The Nature of Creativity: Contemporary Psychological Perspectives.* Cambridge: Cambridge University Press

Dewey, J. (1958). *Art as Experience.* New York: Capricorn Books.

Goulding, C., Shankar, A. and Canniford, R. (2013). Learning to be tribal: Facilitating the formation of consumer tribes. *European Journal of Marketing, 47*(5/6), 813–22.

Hesmondhalgh, D. (2010). User-generated content, free labour and the cultural industries. *Ephemera, 10*(3/4), pp. 267–84.

Hills, M. (2002). *Fan Cultures.* London: Routledge.

Hippel, E. von. (2006). *Democratizing Innovation.* Cambridge, MA: Cambridge MIT Press.

Hyde, L. (2006). Jefferson's Taper: How American revolutionaries imagined cultural wealth. Conference paper at the Political Economy Research Institute, University of Massachusetts, Amherst, MA, 6 March 2006.

Katz, E. and Lazarsfeld, P. (1955). *Personal Influence.* Glencoe, IL: The Free Press.

Keen, A. (2011). *The Cult of the Amateur: How Blogs, MySpace, YouTube and the Rest of Today's User-Generated Media Are Destroying Our Economy, Our Culture and Our Values.* New York: Doubleday.

Kelly, O. (1984). *Community, Art and the State: Storming the Citadels.* London: Comedia.

Kline, N. (1999). *Time to Think: Listening to Ignite the Human Mind.* London: Cassell.

Lessig, L. (2015). *Free Culture: How Big Media Uses Technology and the Law to Lock Down Culture and Control Creativity.* New English edition. Oslo: Petter Reinholdtsen.

Liebes, T. and Katz, E. (1990). *The Export of Meaning: Cross-Cultural Readings of Dallas*. New York: Oxford University Press.

Løvlie, A. and Waern, A. (2022). *Hybrid Museum Experiences: Theory and Design*. Amsterdam: Amsterdam University Press.

Maitlis, S. and Sonenshein, S. (2010) Sensemaking in crisis and change: Inspiration and insights from Weick (1988). *Journal of Management Studies*, *47*(3), pp. 551–80.

Nisbett, M. and Walmsley, B. (2016). The romanticization of charismatic leadership in the arts. *The Journal of Arts Management, Law, and Society*, *46*(1), pp. 2–12.

Pine, B.J. and Gilmore, J. (1999). *The Experience Economy: Work Is Theatre and Every Business a Stage*. Boston, MA: Harvard Business Press.

Rifkin, J. (2000). *The Age of Access: The New Culture of Hypercapitalism Where All of Life Is a Paid-for Experience*. New York: Tarcher Putnam.

Senge, P. (2006). *The Fifth Discipline: The Art and Practice of the Learning Organisation*. London: Random House.

Søderberg, A. (2003). Sensegiving and sensemaking in integration processes. In: Czarniawska, B. and Gagliardi, P. (eds.), *Narratives We Organize by*. Amsterdam/Philadelphia: John Benjamins, pp. 1–45.

Srnicek, N. (2017). *Platform Capitalism*. Cambridge: Polity.

Verganti, R. (2009). *Design-Driven Innovation: Changing the Rules of Competition by Radically Innovating What Things Mean*. Boston, MA: Harvard Business Press.

Weick, K. (1995). *Sensemaking in Organizations*. Thousand Oaks/London: Sage.

Zuboff, S. (2019). *The Age of Surveillance Capitalism: The Fight for a Human Future at the New Frontier of Power*. New York: PublicAffairs.

5 Leading for innovation
Connecting theories to practice

Chapters 2–4 have sketched three models of cultural management. Whilst each model developed out of specific contexts – political, economic and technological – the chronology is not clear-cut. In this final chapter, I will argue that the models coexist – and that cultural managers will need to combine different techniques rather than embracing one or another.

Considering how creativity and innovation operate in the cultural and creative industries, this chapter will show how leaders must adapt to different stages in the innovation process. Situated theories of leadership (Hersey and Blanchard 1972) argue that there is no single best-practice model of leadership. Effective leadership will respond to the situation of the organisation and of the follower. For example, in the early stages of an organisation, and with a relatively low level of commitment and expertise among the followers, leaders will need to be more directive. For a mature organisation where followers have high levels of expertise and motivation, the role of the leader shifts to coaching and supporting rather than directing. Talking about leadership rather than management also takes us back to one of the fundamental challenges of cultural management – in a sector where creative people are highly self-motivated, with highly specialised skills, is there a useful role for a leader? Should the leader just step aside, or busy themselves in the back office with operational, administrative tasks? The usual metaphor for managing creativity is 'herding cats', implying that the leader's task is impossible. But this chapter will argue that innovation and creativity can be 'led' – we just need to situate leadership in the right way (Caust 2018, 23–39).

The innovation process requires quite different capabilities at different stages in its operation. Innovation is usually defined as applied creativity – taking a creative idea and applying this to a specific problem in order to effect change. Because I want to emphasise the multiple

DOI: 10.4324/9781003009184-5

stages of creative thinking, this more extensive definition of innovation will capture a wider set of management strategies.

Switching the focus from 'management' to 'leadership' will focus discussion on the strategic aspects of cultural management rather than the everyday operational aspects. This is not to diminish the importance of operational management. A strategy is pointless without a plan to implement it. But those operational aspects are often best approached pragmatically, learned by doing and shaped by experience rather than any theoretical model. Operational and practical tasks, like people management and the human side of management, are difficult to teach formally. Consequently, they do not feature highly in business curricula, despite their undoubted importance. On cultural management courses, practical operational skills are typically delivered through work placements, despite all of the problems surrounding unpaid internships (exploitation, lack of accountability and lack of clearly definable learning outcomes). Talking about leadership highlights the ideas, strategies and assumptions which lie behind those daily operational decisions and tasks.

So this chapter takes 'Leading for Innovation' as its theme, and will consider how different models of leadership can apply to different stages in the innovation process. The chapter is arranged in three sections, reflecting tropes associated with Cultural Managements 1.0, 2.0 and 3.0, respectively.

Leading for creation

In the cultural and creative industries, where value is only known at the point of consumption, the further we are from the consumer, the higher the uncertainty. The point of origination or ideation is the place of maximum uncertainty where 'nobody knows anything'. At the same time, during this experimental phase, costs are relatively low. Originators of creative and cultural products work iteratively, trying things out, failing, trying again. Not surprisingly, during this pre-production phase, the cultural and creative industries rely upon smaller creative enterprises and individuals. Further down the value chain, as successive investments of time and resources translate the raw idea into a working prototype and then to a marketable product, the uncertainty is somewhat reduced (but never entirely removed). Meanwhile, the costs go up. During this phase of the creative process, the exploitation phase, larger corporations (record labels, film studios, broadcasters and publishers) play an increasingly important role. The differing levels of uncertainty and cost along the value chain help to explain the hollowed-out structure of the

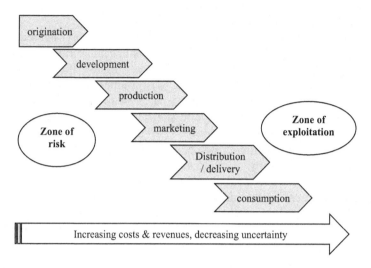

Figure 5.1 Risk and the value chain.

cultural and creative industries, with a large number of very small 'independent' producers orbiting around a handful of very large corporate distributors and publishers. These different levels of risk along the value chain are illustrated in Figure 5.1.

The first phase of the innovation process takes place in the 'zone of risk'. In order to develop a potential idea, it is necessary to take risks and to rely on intuition and energy rather than analysis and planning. In the model of creativity proposed by Graham Wallas (drawing upon the work of Henri Poincaré), this is the phase of 'incubation' and 'illumination' where divergent thinking, spontaneity and irrationality are needed. Other types of thinking will be needed at other stages in the process – the 'preparation' and 'verification' stages demand a more analytical approach. But at this point, with no prior knowledge of future outcomes and high levels of uncertainty, leaders must nurture intuitive, experimental thinking. Figure 5.2 maps the zone of risk/uncertainty and the zone of exploitation/certainty onto these different phases in the creative process.

In their influential study of theories of entrepreneurial action, Alvarez and Barney (2007) make a distinction between 'discovery' and 'creation'. Discovery theory assumes that opportunities exist, the entrepreneur just needs to discover them; they also need to discover the opportunity before somebody else does, drawing upon their superior

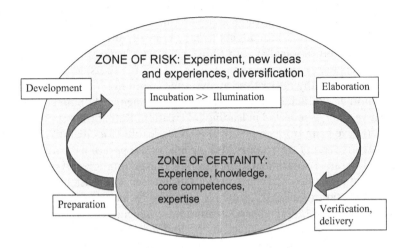

Figure 5.2 Stages in the creative process – between risk and certainty.

expertise, knowledge and 'alertness'. Creation theory assumes that the entrepreneur must create their own opportunities – rather than finding a mountain to climb, the creative entrepreneur must build their own mountain. Expertise and knowledge are less important – rather the creative entrepreneur must be motivated, and must be adaptive, because each action they take will shape the emerging opportunity.

What kind of leadership is needed during this phase of the creative process? Alvarez and Barney argue that leadership for creation will rely on charisma rather than expertise – inspiring the creative team to take actions with no clear outcome or goal. At this experimental stage in the creation process, characterised by problem-finding as much as problem-solving, leaders trust the creative team to take their own risks and make their own decisions. As discussed in Chapter 2, creativity as an intrinsically motivated process requires no external interventions; indeed, extrinsic rewards, threats and evaluations can distract or crowd out intrinsic motivations. Cultural Management 1.0 was accordingly characterised as a non-interventionist approach. Standing outside the creative process, Cultural Management 1.0 aims to manage outcomes, not processes.

As noted in Chapter 2, one of the strengths of Cultural Management 1.0 is the space it provides for intrinsic motivation. But leading for creation requires something more proactive than a pure laissez-faire approach. Transformational leaders seek to build shared purpose and to energise the creative team. Intrinsic motivation cannot be forced, but it can be nurtured through an open, tolerant organisational culture, and by empowering individuals to take control and take risks. These behaviours are associated with transformational leadership or 'leading from the back'. Allowing creative teams to call the shots depends upon trust and empathy rather than analysis and planning.

Another characteristic of Cultural Management 1.0, 'buffering' the creative team, is reflected in leading for creation. Rather than protecting the creative team from commercial realities, leading for creation buffers the creative team from failure. Making mistakes is part of a creative process of iterative experimentation, meaning that adaptation and risk need to be both tolerated and encouraged. This is easier when risk takes place within the 'affordable loss' principle identified by Sarasvathy (2001). By failing fast and failing cheap, creative entrepreneurs can afford to fail often. Leaders can encourage this by limiting financial exposure and setting boundaries within which creative decision-making can run free. As with 'buffering', the creative process is ring-fenced and protected from strategic interventions, allowing the creative team to focus on emerging opportunities rather than potential losses (Kahneman 2012).

The ethos behind this approach to leadership is release rather than control – creating a space and culture within which creative opportunities can be maximised. Such an approach is effective in generating ideas, but this is only one stage in the innovation process. 'Brainstorming' follows a similar logic, deferring idea assessment in order to maximise idea generation. Brainstorming is criticised because whilst suspension of judgement may generate more ideas, it may not generate better ideas. For brainstorming to work effectively, it needs to be framed by a more analytical approach setting out the problem to be solved and the parameters within which solutions can be explored. In Wallas' classic four-stage model of creativity, this is the 'preparation' stage before 'incubation' and 'illumination'. The fourth stage, 'verification', again requires a more deliberate, rational approach in order to assess, filter and select the ideas that have been generated. In other words, release and control alternate through the innovation process – it is not enough to pursue one or other approach in isolation.

In organisational contexts, timing the transition point from one stage to the next becomes critical. In Rosabeth Moss Kanter's model of organisational innovation, the ability to mobilise resources and support around emergent ideas will be crucial to their success (Kanter 1988). Intervene too soon and the judgement will be premature – intervene too late and the idea may have withered on the vine. And, of course, switching between leadership styles demands a creative mindset – the ability to bridge between apparently contradictory frames of reference.

When it comes to idea generation – the 'creation' or ideation stage in the innovation journey – leaders need to coach rather than control. They need to set a culture that encourages risk and empowers experimentation. A lot depends here on the relationships within the group. In their discussion of 'project-based enterprise' in the film industry, DeFillippi and Arthur highlight the importance of 'relationships' and 'dialogue' as an alternative to more hierarchical approaches to decision-making (DeFillippi and Arthur 1998, 135). Establishing these relationships and building trust becomes a prerequisite for cultural leadership, especially in the cultural sector (Morley and Silver 1977). Rather than directing or controlling organisational culture, Daymon argues that leaders of cultural organisations enable cultural values to emerge from below based on shared professional norms and values, and provide a focal point for these cultural values to be shared and legitimised (Daymon 2000).

Academic literature shows approaches to transformational leadership, especially 'leading from below', being pioneered and piloted in creative organisations – in film, animation and theatre – in organisations like Pixar, Cirque du Soleil and the BBC (Catmull 2008; Kim and Mauborgne 2005; Schlesinger 2010). Where Cultural Management 1.0 imported traditional management methods and hierarchies into cultural organisations, leading for creation reverses that trend. A light-touch, culturally driven, non-hierarchical approach to leadership is being developed in the cultural sector and redefining ideas about leadership in mainstream traditional organisations.

Leading for creation is the spark which initiates the innovation journey. Moving from idea generation to the development and application of creative ideas takes us further along the value chain into the later stages in the innovation process – idea testing, filtering, verification and application. Here, more directive approaches to leadership become important. This becomes especially important in order to consolidate and build from the initial creative idea into a viable creative enterprise.

Leading for connection

If innovation was simply about generating innovative ideas, we could stop with 'leading for creation'. But in order to meet the criteria for creativity, innovative ideas also need to be valuable or 'fit for purpose'. This requires a number of further inputs and connections, bringing in additional resources and skills. Because the value of an innovation is relative to its application, the leader must also connect the innovative solution to a specific context. Leading for connection takes a more active role than leading for creation, brokering connections between different individuals and competences, and connecting along the value chain between inputs, outcomes and applications. As with Cultural Management 2.0, this is a more strategic and 'joined up' approach to leadership which assumes that creative inputs and commercial applications are part of a continuum, not in opposition. And if leading for creation is more inwardly directed – empathetic, intuitive, person-based – leading for connection is more outward facing, and more focused on processes than people.

The idea of 'stages' in the creative process is useful because it highlights the different types of thinking required (and, by extension, the diversity of people participating in these stages). Wallas' classic formulation of Preparation–Incubation–Illumination–Verification highlights the interchange between rational and imaginative thinking needed to meet the criteria of both novelty *and* value (Figure 5.3). Variations on the model include additional phases of evaluation and elaboration. Moving from creativity to innovation, a further set of steps is added including application and production – the idea needs to be given material form in order to be protected as intellectual property (copyrights, patents and trademarks). Each of these steps has its own requirements in terms of skills and resources.

In reality, the process is more like a loop than a linear progression (see Figure 5.2 for a circular model), with steps going backwards as well as forwards depending on progress. This iterative process is implicit in phases of 'verification' and 'evaluation' – if the idea is not working,

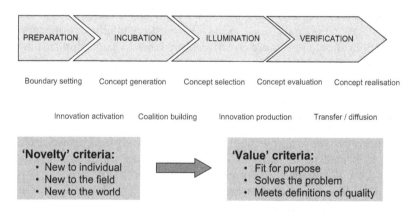

Figure 5.3 Stages in the creative process, from novelty to value.

the process circles back to an earlier version or even starts again from scratch. This circular process is, of course, part of any entrepreneurial journey – try, fail, rethink and try again. But the creative process must also find a balance between 'novelty' and 'value', between something imaginative and unheralded and something that fits with the framework of problem and solution. So, the circling back is also an attempt to rebalance between apparently contradictory requirements and inputs.

In order to manage this process of development and redevelopment, the leader has to dial up and dial down different emphases and inputs. Michael Kirton's classification of 'adapters' and 'innovators' (Kirton 1984) highlights the different, oppositional tendencies in play. In an engineering project, the innovators might be pushing for novel solutions and for radical change; meanwhile, the adapters might be trying to understand how to apply that novelty to solve a specific problem. The leader will need to bridge between the adapters and innovators in the team. So, 'leading for connection' will involve balancing these different tendencies, and ensuring that the tension between different ways of thinking is productive rather than mutually destructive.

In the cultural and creative industries, skills and roles are highly specialised; this job specialisation is taken further with the introduction of digital technologies of production and distribution. Role specialisation is reflected in the fragmentation of cultural production into small specialist teams and individuals collaborating on temporary projects (Grabher 2004). The structure of the cultural and creative industries is 'post-Fordist' with networks of specialists replacing unitary organisations and much of the work happening outside or between traditional workplaces (Eikhof 2013). Joining up these different specialisations into a coherent system – a circle or constellation rather than a production line – is the essence of 'leading for connection'.

As well as managing the internal dynamics of the creative process, leaders must also connect with external constituencies and stakeholders. The two criteria for creativity, novelty and value must not only be reconciled internally, they must be framed externally. The novelty and the value of an idea will always depend on a specific context – social, economic, cultural and political. The leader needs to catch the context in which the work is to be received and find the right mix of novelty and value to fit the purpose. For example, a game that is a sequel to an existing franchise or based on a film will not require the same level of novelty as a stand-alone release. The value of a TV show or film will be relative to global and national trends, political events and economics – all of which must be anticipated during pre-production, several years before the release date. The vagaries of the art market and the posthumous rise and fall in artistic reputations offer another stark reminder that value (and novelty) are always relative to a particular time and place.

Having considered the internal connections and compromises needed for the creative process, the external connections to markets and audiences, the third layer of connections the leader needs to make is between one project and the next. The cultural and creative industries rely on a small number of successful projects to bankroll a high proportion of failures. This can lead to a project-focused mindset, because each project (film, album, novel or advertising campaign) will be different and will require a different combination of inputs. Replicating past success is notoriously difficult – sequels can provide some continuity, but in all but a handful of cases there is a law of diminishing returns. To move from a successful project to a successful organisation, leaders have to be able to connect together multiple projects, making trade-offs between different levels of risk, investment and longevity. In an industry where each product is a one-off prototype, the leader must attempt to provide some continuity at the organisational level in values, customer expectations and collective identity.

Leading for connection takes us past a person-based view of creativity towards a systems-based view (Csikszentmihalyi 1988). The meaning and value of creative ideas depend upon the ecosystem within which they are both produced and consumed. According to a systems theory of creativity, this relates to the 'domain' and the 'field', respectively – creativity is rarely an individual act, and both individuals and groups produce their work based on a 'domain' – a set of shared understandings, traditions, skills and knowledge embedded in communities and subcultures. Once completed, the work is disseminated and filtered through a 'field' of institutions, markets and gatekeepers. The domain is where the product is originated, the field is where it is developed and distributed. Novelty is measured against the domain – the extent to which the creative product deviates from norms, values and traditions prevalent in the domain at the time. Value depends upon the field – with various intermediaries and filters shaping the audience's response to the work and their perception of its value.

How might we characterise 'leading for connection'? Is it associated with any particular skills or aptitudes? Compared to 'leading for creation', leading for connection requires a more analytical mindset. In order to make connections between different capabilities within in the team, to connect the team to the 'meaningful outside', to build continuity between teams and projects will require a depth of knowledge and understanding. It would help too, if the leader had some knowledge of the field/domain in which they are operating. All of this points towards a more cognitive approach than the more emotionally intelligent approach of leading for creation. It might also suggest somebody with a range of experiences and contacts across the relevant sector. The risk here though is focusing too much on traits like experience, knowledge and connections and not enough on behaviours – analysis, seeing the bigger picture, communicating outside specialisms.

One way of conceptualising these leadership behaviours is Karl Weick's theory of storytelling and sensemaking, considered in Chapter 4. Weick (1995) suggests that leaders make sense of the organisation and the world around it by providing a compelling narrative that pulls together different elements – characters, plots, episodes and scenarios – and allows members of the organisation or team to feel part of a bigger story. This seems especially relevant to cultural and creative organisations where the nature of the work means that many individuals don't see beyond their own specific task or role. Including these individual contributions in a larger narrative empowers them to feel connected and appreciated, especially when they are perhaps not in a more visible, starring role.

A second way of conceptualising leading for connection is to refer to ideas of bisociation, paradox and contradiction. Leading for connection bridges between different contributions, contexts and mindsets. Some of these elements are in opposition. For example, the pursuit of novelty can work against the pursuit of value, and vice versa. The creative work of inventing and developing an imaginative idea can clash with the need to evaluate and apply this idea to solve a problem. According to psychological theories, creative processes encompass divergent and convergent thinking, intuition and analysis, imagination and rationality, external constraints and internal objectives. Frank Barron's 'tolerance for contradictions', Howard Gardner's theory of multiple intelligences, Steinberg's cognitive domains, Koestler's bisociation theory all underline that creative thinking involves the reconciliation of opposing or contradictory ideas and processes (Barron 1958; Gardner 1984; Sternberg 1988; Koestler 1976). Translating these psychological connections to an organisational setting, leaders have to facilitate switches between different ways of thinking and between different individuals, groups and departments in the organisation, making sense of one side to another.

Over and above these theoretical models, leading for connection is based on aligning people, tasks and processes. Breaking down a task or project into its component parts, then mapping these onto the capabilities and synergies within the team, calls for an analytical understanding of the creative process and an emotional, empathetic understanding of creative individuals. Unlocking the right combination will remove a lot of the friction and anxiety in the team and allow the process to flow; failing to find the right alignment will mean that even a highly motivated team and inspiring leader will struggle to get results.

So, leading for connection will require an ability to switch between thinking styles, logics and frames of reference. It will require some understanding of the bigger picture of a creative project, team or organisation beyond the individual contribution. And it will require an ability to communicate that bigger picture to others and implicate them in a shared narrative, which inspires future purpose and commitment.

In many cultural and creative organisations, 'leadership' is no longer the preserve of a single leader – precisely because leadership must bridge between opposing tendencies, it may well be distributed through the organisation or shared across a leadership team. Jo Caust has described an 'organic' model of collaborative leadership in the arts where leadership roles are interchangeable (Caust 2018, 107–26). For this to work, each individual still needs to be committed to understanding and communicating the bigger picture and to be tolerant of opposing or contradictory viewpoints. At the Royal Shakespeare Company in the 2000s, leadership of the organisation was modelled on the theatrical principles of ensemble – a group of people with a shared understanding of the goal, trusting each other to learn from mistakes rather than blaming each other, a unifying set of values and vision which cut across every aspect of the company, from performers to marketing and admin staff. Leadership was distributed across the ensemble rather than invested in one person – and the nominal leaders, the artistic director and CEO, operated as a team, not a hierarchy (Hewison et al. 2010).

Of the three models of leadership considered in this chapter, leading for connection is the one closest to conventional leadership as it is taught in business schools. These behaviours and capabilities - being systematic, analytical, empathetic, bridging between different viewpoints and subcultures, delegating and sharing tasks rather than trying to micromanage –would be familiar territory for a typical MBA student. Yet in the cultural and creative industries, this systematic approach to leadership is less familiar precisely because it takes a collective, multifaceted view of creativity as the aggregate of many contributions rather than a single stroke of individual genius. Leading for connection picks up where leading for creation ended, taking the raw ideas and talents at the start of the creative process and tracking this through the many collective inputs needed to turn an idea into a reality.

Leading for reinvention

Chapter 4 argued that innovation is not a self-contained process. Innovative products and processes have an afterlife, with reinventions taking the original idea in sometimes unexpected directions. 'Open innovation' and 'open source' describe an attempt to harness this energy, releasing 'beta' products as a kind of work in progress which users then customise and adapt through a process of co-creation. What started as a way of removing bugs in software development is now an accepted business strategy, involving consumers in the production process. One of the pioneers in this field, Lego, now has a fully fledged co-creation platform, Lego Ideas, where an online community of fans can collaborate with the company to initiate and evaluate new ideas.

In the cultural and creative industries, where successful products are outnumbered by a high proportion of failures, trying to extract additional value from an innovative product is especially important. Secondary release windows, sequels, cross-media franchises (the game of the film of the book) all extend the product life cycle, opening up new markets and new sources of revenue (which can in turn be used to bankroll 'leading for creation' at the start of the product life cycle, where investments and the value of the product are unpredictable). In the cultural and creative industries, time to market (the time taken to create and then realise a product) is long, whereas time in market is notoriously short. Consumers are looking out for the next new thing, and many products and services are 'experiential', used up in the experience of consumption. Producing a film or writing a book is measured in years; watching or reading the outcome is measured in hours. Allowing space for successful products to be renewed and relaunched is thus an essential part of the business model.

As described in Chapter 4, fan cultures have been an important source of reinvention in the cultural and creative industries. Of course, digital technologies and the sophistication and inventiveness of audiences have played a significant part in this emergence. But it is also a conscious strategy among many cultural and creative businesses to foster these fan cultures, through a more permissive approach to intellectual 'property', through building customer engagement on digital platforms, by teasing out themes and ideas most likely to engage fans ('fan service'). This strategic attempt to foster consumer co-creation is one part of 'leading for reinvention'.

Many of today's cultural products are explicitly designed for co-creation. In games, the architecture of an 'open world' game invites the player to explore and experience that world at their own pace, pursuing their own interests and satisfactions. Even a more straight-forward quest or combat game allows the player multiple routes to the desired outcome (different ways to win). Co-creation is built into the gameplay. More 'closed' formats – a book, a film, a piece of music – still allow the audience to experience the product in multiple ways. From a media theory perspective, there are no 'closed' texts – all texts are to some extent open. Even propaganda can be subverted, from the graffiti mocking billboards to the memes which ridicule grandiose statements and gestures in blockbuster movies. Leading for reinvention is an attempt to build in those subversive features as part of the product design.

What does this mean for leadership? As noted in Chapter 4, it requires a certain humility and a concession of power. The leader does not claim to know all of the answers, allows that a fan might have a more creative interpretation of a cultural product than the person who created it, allows that a brand might be subverted and reinvented by its consumers. The example of games design also demonstrates that there is a more active, strategic element to leading for innovation – not just giving permission for users to co-create, but trying to engineer spaces and opportunities for their involvement.

The community arts movement, subsequently rebranded as partici-patory arts and rebooted as cultural democracy, highlights another aspect of leading for innovation. The aim of the animateur or partici-patory arts worker in a community arts project is to facilitate a creative process among others rather than to lead from the front. This requires a kind of generosity and self-restraint – the 'leader' has to inspire others to lead. Participants may feel they lack professional skills, they may aspire to an orthodox version of professional 'quality' and depre-cate their own efforts as amateurish. Beyond the project's participants, audiences and funders may also demand 'professional' quality in the outcomes, pressing both the participants and the project leader to focus on outcomes rather than trusting in the process. Resisting these external pressures, overcoming the participants' self-doubt and restraining their desire to impose their own received ideas of quality and profession-alism, require a particular type of leadership.

Matt Peacock is the founder of Arts and Homelessness International, a UK charity working with homeless people and charities to initiate art-istic projects, raise awareness and influence policy. He describes his lead-ership style as 'giving away power' – building trust and confidence and encouraging others to take a lead. He also believes that leadership cap-abilities take many forms – and values like resilience and empathy might be as important in this type of work as 'charisma' or 'strategic vision'. This idea of 'leading from below', which has inspired community arts work for more than 50 years, is a key component in leading for reinvention.

Peacock's leadership style also embraces the idea of 'vulnerable leadership'. This has been developed in Brené Brown's books and workshops on leadership, as discussed in Chapter 4. By showing weakness and admitting failure, vulnerable leaders build more authentic relationships and give others permission to take risks and experiment. They also create a space for new initiatives – and for new leaders. By saying 'I don't know how to do this', the vulnerable leader invites somebody else to take up the baton.

Applying vulnerable leadership to 'leading for reinvention', the vulnerable leader provides a platform for the next generation of leaders to take up the innovation cycle. The next phase of innovation might come from a group of inexperienced, junior co-workers coming up with a risky new initiative. It might come from fans playing with a product in order to reinvent it. Charles Handy based his model of organisational growth on a sigmoid curve (Handy 1994). Just as the organisation begins to hit the peak of its potential, a second organisational life cycle is launched, based on a new initiative, new people, new ideas. The counterintuitive idea behind Handy's model is that the organisation has to change *before* it reaches the peak of its success – if it delays to the point where organisational growth has reached a plateau or begun to decline, the resources, confidence and motivation to initiate a new direction will have dissipated.

On paper, Handy's model makes perfect sense. Of course we should start to change before it's too late. Of course we should try to reinvent the organisation, project or product from a position of strength, not delay until we are facing a losing battle against declining resources, markets and confidence. Emotionally, the sigmoid curve model is more challenging. In effect Handy argues that the right time to change direction is just at the point where we feel we are most successful, when we are at the peak of our powers. At this point, we throw everything away and start again. That requires a sacrifice from the incumbent leadership, especially the founder or owner, and an enormous investment of trust (and finance) in the next generation of leadership needed to take the organisation forwards.

In the cultural and creative industries, this kind of redirection is recognised as a necessary part of the creative process. It is commonly accepted that the first idea is rarely the best idea, and just because an idea or project has been invested in and supported is no reason to continue down the same path. Screenwriters use the phrase 'kill your babies' to describe the painful decision to delete a scene or character that they have lovingly created, because it is no longer viable or relevant to the larger scenario or story. In the creative sector, sacrifice and reinvention, deleting drafts and starting again, are all part of the creative process. Handy's sigmoid curve is actually more like a succession of curves or loops, each one a new version or iteration, with the project, organisation or product evolving gradually through successive reinventions.

Reinvention fits with a Darwinian theory of creativity, where progress is the result of blind variation and selective retention (Simonton 1999, 2011). Rather than claiming to know the way forward, the leader creates a space in which 'blind variations' – experimental projects – are tolerated and encouraged even though few will survive. A handful of these experiments will be successful, and these will be retained, developed and grown. Yet even as these successful versions emerge, there will be a continuing investment in future 'blind' projects, with equally uncertain prospects. This is the business model of the film industry and the music industry. But again, the emotional component to this is sometimes overlooked. The biggest, most successful project must be exploited to invest in a host of potential usurpers – many of whom will disparage the hand that feeds them. At least 90% of those investments will fail – this was the business model which so baffled Guy Hands and his Terra Firma investment company when they took over EMI – why waste all this money on failed bands, why not continue to exploit the back catalogue of the Beatles or Adele? The answer lies in the sigmoid curve – eventually the curve will decline, or even worse the golden goose will run away to join a rival – as happened with one of EMI's prize assets, Radiohead, shortly after Hands' takeover. Nothing lasts forever – the music industry is a moving target, not 'terra firma'.

From a leadership perspective, leading for reinvention involves risk and trust. Allowing those inside or outside the business to initiate new ideas carries a high risk of failure. Rather than Handy's pivotal crossover to a new direction, leaders can mitigate that risk by initiating multiple potential sigmoid curves, only a few of which will come to fruition. Each initiative means handing over resources and control to an untried project and team, trusting them with a new venture, tolerating failure – but by making this a regular investment rather than a single reinvention, the failures can be relatively quick and cheap, ideas can be recycled and lessons learned. Spreading risk means trusting others and not attempting to impose one's own vision and values – the antithesis of charismatic leadership.

This takes us to the core of leading for reinvention, the acceptance that others may know better than the leader how to develop a new project or idea. As with Handy's sigmoid curve, there is a generational aspect to this – the older, established leaders handing the baton to the young, allowing them to run their own race. This is a kind of resignation or sacrifice, what Matt Peacock calls 'giving away power'. In the cultural and creative industries, it might mean handing over a cherished brand to fans, allowing them to hack, remix and reinvent the original. It might mean giving up 'ownership' of intellectual property in order to cultivate 'influence', trusting in the wisdom of the crowd instead of the years of experience and expertise painfully acquired and invested in the core business. There is a sacrificial, self-destructive element to this – but as with religious myths of sacrifice, giving away power means regenerating and reinventing something even more powerful and valuable.

The endgame of leading for reinvention is the resignation of the leader – the leader becomes the follower, the followers become the new leaders. The ultimate achievement of leadership is to allow others to lead.

This chapter has followed a situational theory of leadership, in which models of leadership are adapted to the situation of leader and follower. Considering the process of innovation, three approaches of leadership have been applied to three successive stages in the innovation process. Leading for creation follows a model of transformational leadership, which aims to inspire and motivate the team to generate new ideas. Leading for connection is more systematic, concerned especially with the alignment of abilities, resources and tasks across a creative team or project, recognising that innovation will draw on multiple inputs. Leading for reinvention uses vulnerable leadership and a concession of control in order to allow others to lead. According to the situational model, changing models of leadership reflect changing roles of the follower, from experimental, self-motivated individualism to collective ownership and teamwork, to the point where the follower becomes the new leader.

The purpose of this chapter has been to show how different approaches to management and leadership can apply to different scenarios and tasks. The focus has been on an evolving process of innovation over time, but variations could also be applied in other dimensions – different approaches to managing projects across a portfolio, or adapting to different media, or to different markets. Situational leadership insists that there is no 'best-practice' model – each situation will be different. Leaders and managers must be eclectic in their approach.

The evolution of leadership across different phases of innovation mirrors the evolution of cultural management over 50 years of practice.

'Evolution' suggests that the latest, most evolved model will be the most advanced and progressive. There is an element of truth to this – Cultural Management 3.0 and 'leading for reinvention' might seem the best response to our current historic situation, where fans, tribes and users are increasingly powerful, where notions of quality and excellence are challenged by postmodern scepticism, where value and purpose are increasingly contingent and unpredictable. But to paraphrase William Gibson, the future may be here but it is not evenly distributed. There will be times when Cultural Management 1.0 (leading for creation) or Cultural Management 2.0 (leading for connection) will be better suited to our present situation, and there will be situations where 'leading for reinvention' is absolutely the wrong approach. As managers and leaders, we need to be eclectic. And by understanding some of the assumptions, historic conditions and scenarios which lie behind different models of management and leadership, we can recognise their imperfections as well as their strengths, and make a more informed choice about which kind of manager or leader each of us wants to be.

References

Alvarez, S. and Barney, J. (2007). Discovery and creation: Alternative theories of entrepreneurial action. *Strategic Entrepreneurship Journal*, *1*(1/2), pp. 11–26.

Barron, F. (1958). The psychology of imagination. *Scientific American*, *199*(3), pp. 251–66.

Catmull, E. (2008). *How Pixar Fosters Collective Creativity*. Boston, MA: Harvard Business School Publishing.

Caust, J. (2018). *Arts Leadership in Contemporary Contexts*. Abingdon: Routledge.

Csikszentmihalyi, M. (1988). Society, culture, and person: A systems view of creativity. In: Sternberg, R.J. (ed.), *The Nature of Creativity: Contemporary Psychological Perspectives*. Cambridge: Cambridge University Press, pp. 325–39.

Daymon, C. (2000). Leadership and emerging cultural patterns in a new television station. *Studies in Cultures, Organizations and Societies*, *6*(2), pp. 169–96.

DeFillippi, R.J. and Arthur, M.B. (1998). Paradox in project–based enterprise: The case of film making. *California Management Review*, *40*(2), pp. 125–39.

Eikhof, D.R. (2013). Transorganisational work and production in the creative industries. In: Bilton, C. and Cummings, S. (eds.), *Handbook of Management and Creativity*. Cheltenham: Edward Elgar Publishing, pp. 275–97.

Gardner, H. (1984). *Frames of Mind: The Theory of Multiple Intelligences*. London: Heinemann.

Grabher, G. (2004). Learning in projects, remembering in networks? Communality, sociality, and connectivity in project ecologies. *European Urban and Regional Studies*, *11*(2), pp. 103–23.

Handy, C. (1994): The sigmoid curve. *The Empty Raincoat: Making Sense of the Future*. London: Hutchison, pp. 49–64.

Hersey, P. and Blanchard, K.H. (1972). *Management of Organizational Behavior Utilizing Human Resources*. Englewood Cliffs, NJ: Prentice-Hall.

Hewison, R., Holden, J. and Jones, S. (2010). *All Together: A Creative Approach to Organisational Change*. London: Demos.

Kahneman, D. (2012). *Thinking Fast and Slow*. London: Penguin.

Kanter, R.M. (1988). When a thousand flowers bloom: Structural, collective and social conditions for innovation in organization. *Research in Organizational Behaviour*, *10*, pp. 123–67.

Kim, W.C. and Mauborgne, R. (2005). *Blue Ocean Strategy: How to Create Uncontested Market Space and Make the Competition Irrelevant*. Harvard, MA: Harvard Business School Press.

Kirton, M. (1984). Adapters and innovators: Why new initiatives get blocked. *Long Range Planning*, *17*(2), 137–43.

Koestler, A. (1976). *The Act of Creation*. London: Hutchinson.

Morley, E and Silver, A. (1977). A film director's approach to managing creativity. *Harvard Business Review* 55(2), pp. 59–70

Sarasvathy, S.D. (2001.) Causation and effectuation: Toward a theoretical shift from economic inevitability to entrepreneurial contingency. *Academy of Management Review*, *26*(2), pp. 243–63.

Schlesinger, P. (2010). 'The most creative organization in the world'? The BBC, 'creativity' and managerial style. *International Journal of Cultural Policy*, *16*(3), pp. 271–85.

Simonton, D.K. (1999). Creativity as blind variation and selective retention: Is the creative process Darwinian? *Psychological Inquiry*, *10*, 309–28.

Simonton, D.K. (2011). Creativity and discovery as blind variation: Campbell's (1960) BVSR model after the half-century mark. *Review of General Psychology*, *15*(2), pp. 158–74.

Sternberg, R. (1988). A three-facet model of creativity. In: Sternberg, R. J. (ed.), *The Nature of Creativity: Contemporary Psychological Perspectives*. Cambridge: Cambridge University Press, pp. 125–47.

Weick, K. (1995). *Sensemaking in Organisations*. Thousand Oaks, CA: Sage.

Index

Printed in the United States
by Baker & Taylor Publisher Services